Marketing in Developing Nations

The developing markets of Africa, Asia and the Middle East are quickly becoming the future of world economic and trade development. They are affluent in terms of population, resources and market expansion, with rising interests from the EU, United States and multi-national corporations in the region. It is therefore imperative for the academic and global business communities to have an accurate picture of the peculiarities of marketing practices, developments and consumer experiences in these developing markets.

This book presents contemporary cases across Africa, Asia and the Middle East to aid the global understanding of both market and consumer behaviours across the regions and equally provide robust knowledge to approach the markets with strategic responses. A unique characteristic of the African economy and the other regional markets like Middle East and Asia is that they might have one global business outlook for non-citizens and non-residents, but the internal structure and market behaviours quite reveal that they are different and diverse in terms of culture, socialisation, religion, technology assimilation, economic capacity etc., which invariably affect market behaviours, buying decisions and consumer behavioural patterns and decisions in each market.

This edited collection will bring together a comprehensive assembly of cases considering these diverse characteristics to provide foresight for marketing strategy, policy and decision-making. *Marketing in Developing Nations* will aid researchers and upper-level students looking to further understand the specifics of marketing in these regions while also offering real-life examples to stimulate further research and insight for global business.

Ayodele C. Oniku is an associate professor in the Department of Business Administration (marketing unit) at the University of Lagos, Nigeria.

Routledge Studies in Marketing

This series welcomes proposals for original research projects that are either single or multi-authored or an edited collection from both established and emerging scholars working on any aspect of marketing theory and practice and provides an outlet for studies dealing with elements of marketing theory, thought, pedagogy and practice.

It aims to reflect the evolving role of marketing and bring together the most innovative work across all aspects of the marketing 'mix' – from product development, consumer behaviour, marketing analysis, branding, and customer relationships, to sustainability, ethics and the new opportunities and challenges presented by digital and online marketing.

For more information about this series, please visit: www.routledge.com/Routledge-Studies-in-Marketing/book-series/RMKT

Marketing in Developing Nations

Contemporary Developments, Cases and Problems in Africa, Asia and the Middle East

Edited by Ayodele C. Oniku

Routledge
Taylor & Francis Group

LONDON AND NEW YORK

First published 2025
by Routledge
4 Park Square, Milton Park, Abingdon, Oxon OX14 4RN

and by Routledge
605 Third Avenue, New York, NY 10158

Routledge is an imprint of the Taylor & Francis Group, an informa business

British Library Cataloguing-in-Publication Data
A catalogue record for this book is available from the British Library

ISBN: 978-1-032-57834-7 (hbk)
ISBN: 978-1-032-57847-7 (pbk)
ISBN: 978-1-003-44127-4 (ebk)

DOI: 10.4324/9781003441274

Typeset in Times New Roman
by Apex CoVantage, LLC

To all those who have chosen Marketing as a career either in the classrooms or in the fields.

Contents

Figures

About the Editor

Ayodele C. Oniku is an associate professor in the Department of Business Administration (Marketing Unit) at the University of Lagos, Nigeria. He is an alumnus of the Department of Economics, Obafemi Awolowo University; the University of Lagos and the Royal Docks Business School, University of East London, UK, respectively. He has experience that spans nearly 30 years in marketing fields in both academic and industry, as well as in African and European markets. He is a co-editor of a compendium titled *Religion and Consumer Behaviour in Developing Nations* and has authored many book chapters. He is a seasoned consultant and coach in marketing and sales fields.

Chapter 11

Contributors

Kwame Adom, Ph.D., is an associate professor of business at the School of Business at Burman University in Lacombe, Alberta. He is the owner and senior consultant of Entrepreneur's Clinique, a business and management consulting firm based in Accra, Ghana. He has a Ph.D. in Management (entrepreneurship focus) from the University of Sheffield Management School, Sheffield, UK; an MBA (finance) from the University of Leicester and a B.Sc. in Planning from Kwame Nkrumah University of Science and Technology. He is an associate member of the Chartered Institute of Marketing (CIM, UK). His research interests draw on experiences from Africa, focusing on micro, small and medium-sized enterprises.

Olamide Akintimehin is a doctoral researcher at the Department of Strategy and Marketing at The Open University, Milton Keynes, UK. Specifically, his current Ph.D. research focuses on the application of gamification within the mobile banking context for financial well-being. His research areas are marketing, luxury branding, entrepreneurship, sustainability and technological innovation. He is a reviewer for international journals like the *Journal of Consumer Marketing*. He worked as a research assistant at Lagos Business School, Pan-Atlantic University, Nigeria, where he contributed to teaching the Business Ethics module on the MBA and executive education programmes.

Ibrahim A. A. AlZahrani is a doctoral student in marketing/international business at the University of Turku, Finland. He is presently working in Saudi Arabia as an innovative healthcare solution expert. Ibrahim was an internationalisation expert and researcher at the University of Turku. He has been known for his work on the European Union Project, and he has more than 20 years of international experience in the industry, which enables him to work in different countries across the globe. He holds a postgraduate diploma in international business from Aalto University, Finland, and master's and bachelor's degrees from Griffith University, Australia.

Robinson A. Bananda, Ph.D., holds a Bachelor of Science (B.Sc.) degree in marketing, a Master of Business Administration (MBA) in marketing and a Doctor of Philosophy (Ph.D.) in marketing. He is currently the HOD of Marketing, a researcher and a senior lecturer at the Department of Marketing, Faculty of

Management Sciences, University of Jos, Nigeria. Dr. Bananda's research interests span e-marketing, service marketing, consumer behaviour, AI, relationship marketing, global marketing and marketing management, among others.

Zainurin B. Dahari, Ph.D., obtained his Ph.D. in marketing from the University of Western Australia (UWA) in 2007. Before joining academia, he gained many years of business experience working as a sales and marketing specialist for organisations in the United States, Malaysia, Japan and Singapore. He has gained excellent teaching experience at the University of Western Australia (UWA), the PSB Academy of Singapore and Unitec, New Zealand. He has held various consultation and thesis supervision responsibilities at the undergraduate, master and Ph.D. levels. He has also done several group research projects, individual research projects and group consulting. Zainurin presently teaches at Higher Colleges of Technology, Al Ain, United Arab Emirates.

Omotola Elatuyi, Ph.D., is a seasoned commercial and strategic planning business leader with significant experience (20+ years) in the fast-moving consumer goods sector across the Middle East and East and West African markets, working in a highly matrixed structure in leading organisations. She led the team that delivered world-class lager under a global beer portfolio and the first brand extension for Global Creme Liquor. She is presently an adjunct lecturer at the University of Lagos Business School.

Saheed A. Gbadegeshin, Ph.D., is a technology commercialisation expert, entrepreneur, entrepreneurship educator and new business development and family business continuity consultant. He worked at the Higher Colleges of Technology, Al-Ain Men's Campus, United Arab Emirates. He is also a dissertation supervisor at Arden University (UK) and a senior research fellow at the Centre for Multidisciplinary Research and Innovation (CEMRI), Finland. He is a member of the Chartered Management Institute (UK). He obtained his doctorate in entrepreneurship from the University of Turku (Finland). He is presently the module leader and technology commercialisation expert at Oxford Brookes University (Global Banking School Campus), London, UK.

Owolabi L. Kuye, Ph.D., is a professor of strategic management and entrepreneurship at the University of Lagos, Nigeria. He is the former dean of the Faculty of Management Sciences, University of Lagos, Nigeria. He was the head of the Department of Business Administration. He was a former coordinator of Masters of Business Administration (MBA) programmes. He is a member of the Academy of Management Nigeria. He is also a member of the Academy of Management (AOM), USA. He was a member of the board of the School of Postgraduate Studies. He is a fellow of the Nigerian Institute of Management (FNIM).

Nnamdi O. Madichie, Ph.D., is a professor of marketing and entrepreneurship at the School of Graduate Studies, University of Kigali, Rwanda. He has researched and published widely on business and management in Africa, with a research focus on the intersection of marketing and entrepreneurship. He has authored and co-authored numerous book chapters and books, including titles like Digital Entrepreneurship in Sub-Saharan Africa (Palgrave/Springer). In addition to serving as a manuscript reviewer for top journals such as the *Journal of Small Business Management* (Wiley), Madichie sits on the editorial board of leading journals such as Management Decision.

Rachid Moustaquim, Ph.D., holds a Ph.D. from the joint programme of the University of Quebec in Montreal, Concordia University, HEC Montreal and McGill University. He has been teaching corporate social responsibility (CSR) and strategy courses at the Department of Strategy and Social and Environmental Responsibility at the Business School of the University of Quebec in Montreal since 2015. He currently teaches at the Higher College of Technology in the UAE. Rachid presently teaches at Higher Colleges of Technology, Al Ain, United Arab Emirates.

Atsu Nkukpornu, Ph.D., is a lecturer in the Department of Entrepreneurship and Agribusiness at Cape Coast Technical University. He has a Ph.D. in Marketing (entrepreneurship focus) and an M.Phil. in Marketing, all from the University of Ghana Business School, a BBA in Marketing from Kwame University of Science and Technology (Garden City University Campus), and an HND in Marketing from Kumasi Technical University. He has over a decade of corporate experience. He is also an entrepreneur and a small business consultant.

Etse Nkukpornu is a lecturer in the Department of Accounting and Finance at Christian Service University College. He holds an M.Phil. (Finance Focus) and an M.Sc. in Economics (Money, Banking and Finance), all from the Kwame Nkrumah University of Science and Technology, Kumasi, Ghana and a BBA in Finance (Money, Banking and Finance) from the Kwame University of Science and Technology (Garden City University Campus). He has over a decade of industry experience. He is a consultant in microbusiness financing.

Kennedy O. Nwagwu holds Ph.D. and Master of Science degrees in marketing and a Bachelor of Science (B.Sc.) degree in business management. He is currently a researcher and a senior lecturer at the Department of Marketing, Faculty of Management Sciences, University of Jos, Nigeria. Dr. Nwagwu's research interests span digital marketing, food marketing, consumer behaviour, marketing communication and marketing management.

Oluwaseun O. Otayemi is a marketing professional who is currently studying for his Ph.D. in marketing at the University of Lagos. Seun is committed to the deepening and demonstration of marketing skills/knowledge with global impacts on businesses, households and national development. Seun's current research work focuses on digital marketing integration and application in SMEs and the informal sector, which dominates many African markets. He is a trainer and consultant in marketing fields with a focus on SMEs and start-ups' strategy development in Nigeria.**Cornelius N. Wukari** is a Ph.D. scholar and a lecturer at the Department of Marketing, Faculty of Management Sciences, University of Jos, Nigeria. He holds a Bachelor of Science (B.Sc.) degree in Business Management and a Master of Business Administration (MBA) in Marketing. His research interests cover marketing, brand management and customer service.

Preface

Undoubtedly, the need to have books on marketing cases and problems that specifically focus on market developments in developing markets is long overdue. The significance of such books is to deepen the knowledge of students – local and international – business managers, marketing practitioners and decision makers outside the market under focus. Equally, it will expose many to the marketing practices, concepts and understandings that prevail in the market. The peculiarities of the developing market define the business decisions and the behavioural patterns of consumers in the markets, and these are fundamental things that many might not understand until they are exposed to information that elicits such information; this is one of the goals that this compendium has achieved.

The African economy and other developing markets like Asia and the Middle East are becoming the world's priceless jewels, and different studies have shown that these markets, especially Africa, Asia and the Middle East, are the future centrepieces of the world economy and trade development. They are well-endowed in terms of population, resources and market expansion, hence the rising interests of the EU, the US and multi-national companies (MNCs) in the regions. The pedagogical focus is to embrace and document market developments with information that will enlighten and illuminate the knowledge of both the academic and global business communities with relevant cases and problems that enunciate the peculiarities of the regions in the areas of environment dynamism, consumer behaviours, market challenges and developments, marketing mix operationalisation and other important marketing practice decisions in the different markets.

One unique characteristic of the African economy and the other regional markets like the Middle East and Asia is that they might have one global business outlook for non-citizens and non-residents, but the internal structure and market behaviours reveal that they are different and diverse in terms of culture, socialisation, religion, technology assimilation, economic capacity etc., which invariably affect market behaviours, buying decisions and consumer behavioural patterns and decisions in each market. These are the potential works for the proposed book to bring to the limelight and the understanding of decision makers and marketing strategists.

The objectives that drive the work are the following:

- To provide, to a greater extent, a comprehensive compilation of marketing cases that are authentically based on and reflect market and consumer behavioural developments across industries, with a focus on marketing practices in African, Asian and Middle Eastern markets.
- To provide detailed development of marketing practices in Africa, Asia and the Middle East in cases and problems to enable teaching that projects developing market peculiarities at both undergraduate and postgraduate levels and in business schools. This will certainly help students understand the diverse markets and, equally, provide tailor-made solutions to marketing issues.
- To reduce reliance on foreign marketing cases to teach prospective and potential managers that are being developed to operate within the developing markets, this will enhance their understanding and sharpen their knowledge of the different developing markets and their characteristics.
- To deepen the knowledge of not only the indigenous managers about the developing markets under focus and consumers but also the existing foreign managers operating in the markets and those who have their eyes on the markets. The book on marketing cases and problems will adequately prepare them for the nature, characteristics and peculiarities of markets and consumers.
- The book on Marketing Cases and Problems will give foresight on the appropriateness of marketing strategies, policies and decisions that are practicable and relevant to the markets under focus. This will further project the potential of marketing practices and their peculiarities in diverse developing markets.
- The book on marketing cases and problems will help students, managers and developing market enthusiasts gain superior knowledge and understanding of the diverse markets in that the nature, characteristics and peculiarities of different facets of the markets will be covered with a focus on sectors and industries.

The Book of Readings will provide more relevant and contemporary information and knowledge on the developments in developing markets, which is becoming important to business education and strategy for entrepreneurs, investors, MNCs and business owners who have nursing interests in developing markets and those who are already making waves in the markets.

With the case studies that cover different marketing fields, we believe that business students across all levels and around the world will find the book invaluable and relevant for erudition and scholarship pursuit.

Acknowledgements

I sincerely appreciate everyone who is involved in this project from the onset until the final stage of the work. Your contribution is priceless, and it means a lot to the marketing fields across the world.

Firstly, I would like to express my greetings to the staff of Routledge, Taylor & Francis Group, most especially Alexandra Atkinson, Yarisa Wahlang Kharbuli and Manjusha Mishra, who were involved with the work from the beginning through the production stages until the end. Thanks greatly.

It is important to appreciate all the companies, business owners, entrepreneurs, business associations, government institutions and departments that gave us all contributors the opportunity to investigate your businesses and provide the necessary information for the work to be a success. Your astute and unwavering support in the course of the work in Ghana, Nigeria, Saudi Arabia, Rwanda and the United Arab Emirates is uncommon and priceless. Thank you all.

Part 1
Product

1 Product Stigmatisation and Product Exaggeration

The Twin Dilemmas of African Consumers

Ayodele C. Oniku

Introduction

The African market, especially the sub-Saharan African market, is known for its large population, teeming young consumers, huge rural dwellers, large low-level educated consumers and weak regulatory institutions. The culmination of the factors does have strong effects on the market propensity to become sophisticated, progressively formal in operations, strong in consumer rights and power, and improved purchase behaviours of the citizenry.

According to the World Bank's Global Economic Prospects (2022), the sub-Saharan African population was documented to be nearly 1.2 billion in 2018 and 1.18 billion in 2021, compared to 227,948 and 869 in the 1960s. This corroborates and represents a Malthusian geometric rise in the population of an economy. On a larger scale, the African population is projected to reach 2.8 billion by 2060 (World Bank's Global Economic Prospects, 2015).

While the population is increasing at that astronomical rate, the GDP of the continent also increases, but not at a rate that can be compared to the other regions of the world. According to the World Bank's Global Economic Prospect (2018), the GDP per capita has improved in sub-Saharan Africa from $31.17 billion in the 1960s to $1.7 trillion and $1.92 trillion in 2020 and 2021, respectively.

According to Statista Economy & Politics (2022), the report beneath shows the GDP per capita of selected African economies:

No	Countries	(GDP) Per Capita in $1,000
1	Morocco	$3.9
2	South Africa	$6.950.43
3	Egypt	$4.5
4	Kenya	$2,111.4
5	Algeria	$4.15
6	Namibia	$4.81
7	Botswana	$7.35
8	Nigeria	$2.43
9	Senegal	$1,436.0
10	Zimbabwe	$1,526.0

(*Continued*)

DOI: 10.4324/9781003441274-2

(Continued)

No	Countries	(GDP) Per Capita in $1,000
11	Ethiopia	$995.67
12	Burkina Faso	$813.01
13	Gabon	$10,280

Source: Statista Economy & Politics (2022)

Importantly, there are a handful of countries with GDP per capita above the benchmark of $10,000, and they are the Seychelles, Equatorial Guinea and Gabon, with GDP per capita of $20,270, $11,260 and $10,280, respectively. On the other hand, the countries with lower GDP per capita are largely found in sub-Saharan Africa, for example the Central Africa Republic (CAR) with $494/52 and Burkina Faso with $813.01, respectively. However, the gap is very great when African GDP per capita is compared to the United States of $69,227, Germany of $48,397.8 and the United Kingdom of $32,887, respectively.

Another pointer to consumer socio-economic well-being is the illiteracy level, which is found to be the highest in the world. According to Statista Economy & Politics (2022), while Africa records 33% illiteracy level, other parts of the world have relatively lower percentages: South Asia (23%), the Arab States (26%), Latin America and Caribbean (6%), East Asia and the Pacific (4%), and Europe and Central Asia (2%), respectively.

Product Exaggeration and Stigmatisation

The cases of product stigmatisation and exaggeration are common phenomena in product acceptance and rejection across the sub-Saharan African market, and each society has its own peculiarities when it comes to adoption, depth and coverage in consumption behaviours. To a large extent, the level of education, prosperity and protection of consumer rights and power by the different regulators, as well as the deployment of marketing communication strategies in the market, will determine the complexity and coverage of product exaggeration and stigmatisation across products.

Importantly, the role of health education in every society plays a greater part in checking and limiting the incidences of product stigmatisation and the occurrence of product exaggeration. This is based on the connection between product abuse, especially edible products, and consumers' health and well-being. Likewise, services can suffer from stigmatisation and exaggeration, and the effects of this on consumers can be explained by the wastage of financial resources and the creation of false hopes for consumers, which eventually happen or manifest at redemption.

Cases of Product Stigmatisation

i. **Vehicle Insurance Policy**: The third-party insurance policy is mostly affected in this case because it is cheaper than the comprehensive policy, hence it is mostly patronised by commercial drivers and many car owners. The foundation of product stigmatisation in the industry can be ascribed to the prevalence of beliefs that vehicle insurance policy is to avoid the arrest of policemen who regularly randomly check vehicle papers and that compensation will not be paid in case of eventuality – an incidence of failed promises. These twin factors entrench the vehicle insurance stigmatisation that happens in many sub-Saharan African markets. Conspicuously, it isn't surprising to see many commercial taxis and some private cars, especially among the low-educated and illiterate demographics, protect their cars with different 'spiritual' ornaments like juju amulets and bracelets; a whole Bible or Quran is kept in the vehicle; or certain inscriptions from the Bible or Quran are boldly written on the vehicles to ward off evil occurrences like accidents or theft. Incidentally, at the occurrence of an accident or theft, the drivers or vehicle owners do not resort to the insurance companies for compensation but take solace in fate. According to industry experts, the dual effects of this are: consumers lose confidence in the industry and patronage of other policies suffers because of the generalisation of 'failed promises' incidence. In addition, unscrupulous and unregistered companies enter the industry, capitalising on many consumers' ignorance and beliefs. Unfortunately, these unscrupulous practitioners' companies do not exist on governments' registered companies lists, but they offer vehicle insurance policies to consumers. Hence, the insurance industry loses millions of dollars every year to these unregistered companies.

ii. **Seasoning:** Medically, it has been reported that a high level of monosodium glutamate (MSG) in processed foods, especially in seasoning, where it forms a sizeable part of raw materials, is not good for human health. The Nigerian Guardian on 13 November 2016 in its health column asserted,

> While some people react to MSG immediately, others feel the effect over time. MSG has been linked to such diseases as, fibromyalgia, liver inflammation, memory problems or migraines. Daily usage of such seasonings is detrimental to the health. People have reported reactions after eating foods with MSG, but researchers have been unable to scientifically prove the allergy.

However, some consumers in sub-Saharan Africa, especially in the West African region, claim that most of the seasonings on the market are not for human consumption because they contain certain 'cloth whitening substance' that is good for stain removal in white clothes. In fact, this claim has greater effects on the brands in white granulated form than the other brands, probably because of their white colour. Many consumers claim that they regularly use them and that they are effective in washing white clothes, and even some consumers claim that they only buy such brands for washing their white clothes and not for cooking. The source of such stigma cannot be verified. Neither the nutritionists nor the industry regulators condemn any of the seasoning brands, especially brands like Ajinomoto and Vedan in the Nigerian market. One might think that the rejection of such brands in the market will be found

only among illiterate and low-educated consumers. Unbelievably, some educated consumers have fallen for such claims in spite of the fact that they
cannot medically verify such claims. And the reason for such rejection is not
far-fetched: 'If it can remove dirty stain in clothes, the whitening substance
might damage intestines.' Many consumers further stress that because of this
factor, they rarely eat outside, especially at parties and some low-class restaurants, because they believe those are food vendors that might use such seasoning brands. Another set of consumers claim that they have resorted to local
and traditional seasoning that is wholly made from African local ingredients,
which they believe has no such chemical composition or materials. Interest-
ingly, all the claims and publicity that most of the seasoning brands that are
greatly affected are made from sugar cane and other organic raw materials
by the manufacturers and industry regulators have not yielded much gain to
obliterate or change the stigma. The questions "is the stigma emanated from
competitors in the industry or poor marketing communication" still remains
unresolved.

iii. **Soda (Carbonated) Drinks**: The rejection faced by soda drinks is multifaceted
in that there is a certain stigma that generally affects all the brands in market,
and some brands are singled out for a certain stigma that leads to rejection or
low patronage in the market. Across the African market, nearly all the global
brands are available, in addition to indigenous brands that are largely local in
distribution and consumption. Thus, it isn't difficult to spot popular brands
like Coke, Fanta, 7Up, Dr Pepper, Sprite, Limca and Schweppes in Nigeria.
The popular local brands are Bigi and La Casera, brands of Rite Foods Ltd.
and The La Casera Company Plc., respectively. An age-long challenge in the
industry in many countries is the connection between soft drinks' regular consumption among adult males and sexual performance. It is common advice
that once a man is sexually mature, regular consumption of soda drinks will
affect his sexual performance. In fact, in some communities, it is a stern warning to married men. The claim stems from an idea that soda drinks contain
a lot of sugar, which can cause piles or haemorrhoids and thereby weaken
men's sexual performance. Another recent development in the market is that
certain brands of soft drinks are very effective in loosening nuts or screws that
are rusty or difficult to unscrew. The practice is very popular among mechanics and technicians; once a nut is difficult to loosen, the common advice is to
pour a few quantities of certain brands of soft drinks on it, and in less than
five minutes it will be easier to loosen with less effort. In fact, many mechanics and technicians have confirmed and corroborated the 'solution,' and this
is fuelling the belief that if what is meant for human consumption can make
hard nuts loosen easily, then it might have serious effects on humans' health.
The corollary in the market is brand rejection and switching brand loyalty
to other brands that are believed not to be 'dangerous' to consumers' health.
Likewise, there is a popular YouTube video that shows that cola drinks are
more effective in cleaning toilet bowls, and many consumers are interpreting
this to believe that consumption of such cola drinks will have serious health

implications. The question remains: Does this mean that there is a chemical reaction between soda, rust screw and toilet bowl that many consumers have misinterpreted as a health hazard, or do the bottlers truly know something that consumers do not know, and the industry regulators keep mute on it? Or, maybe, a question of short-sighted marketing communication and poor labelling issues in product management?

iv. **Sausage:** The fact is that only a few African countries have that sophisticated and well-developed culinary industry, maybe those few countries where the tourism industry is developed, and it provides a veritable source of revenue to the system to cater for the consumption needs of many international tourists. Largely, meat business and consumption in many African economies are limited to the traditional goat, sheep and ram, cattle and chicken, duck (especially in many North African counties) and bush meat (more popular today among rural dwellers). Thus, the processing of meat into different forms like sausage, ham, barbecue, pepperoni, hot dogs and beef jerky is just gaining ground and popularity in many societies and is largely recognised as western styles or menus. The case of sausage is more peculiar because it has been introduced to the confectionery list in many African societies, and the dominant belief is that all sausages are made from pork. Consequently, some consumers avoid eating anything made from pork because the claim is that it is all made from pork. Thus, the Muslim faithful who see it as Haram based on Quranic injunction, certain Christian sects who see it as forbidden based on the event recorded in the Bible passage of Mark 5: 1–16 and the African Traditional Religion practitioners whose deities may forbid it. This claim, to a large extent, is affecting sausage consumption and patronage in both confectionery and the larger culinary industries. It is not strange to see an average African consumer avoid sausage on menu lists in any part of the world, with the exception of those who are well-informed, and in many cases, many seek to find the source of the sausage before patronage. Is this a case of poor food or product education, inadequacy in labelling or the wrong belief that all sausage is made from pork?

Cases From Product Exaggeration

v. **Sex Enhancement:** The penchant to improve sexual performance or indulge in extra sexual intimacy has made many consumers seek different unorthodox and medically unapproved means that they find handy, easily concocted and cheap to obtain. These concoctions or self-made prescriptions are believed to work effectively by many consumers, and they recommend them to others. From there, they become popular and household names among adults, whether married or single. The source or genesis of this cannot be verified, and how it spreads like wildfire is unfathomable. Surprisingly, they are decades old in Nigerian societies. In this category of sex enhancement and sexual pleasure mixtures are stout drink and milk mixture, which many use regularly. Naturally, stout drinks are derived from roasted malt and barley and are black and thick in their physical form. It is a traditional drink from Ireland that has spread across the world. Stout is clearly different from beer because of the inclusion of roasted barley in its formulation and the fact that it has a stronger flavour and higher alcohol content than beer. Thus, stout is more or less another beer but dark in colour because of roasted malt and barley. The imminent question is: What makes a stout beer and milk mixture a good recipe for sex enhancement, but not ordinary lager or a beer and milk mixture? Another mixture in this sex enhancement mixture category is condensed milk and honey. Condensed milk is a category of dairy made from concentrated milk in which about 60% of the water content is removed and sugar is added before it is canned. This is not as popular as the former, but equally effective and accepted among the few people who adopt the mixture. The pertinent question is: Are the manufacturers of these products and brands aware of this exaggerated usage because it isn't stated on the labelling as part of the products' function, usage or application?

vi. **Dandruff, Ringworm and Eczema Treatment:** Dandruff is a condition that causes the skin or scalp to flake, and specifically, it is a fungal infection, and equally bacteria, that is very contagious. Dandruff can be oil-based, dry scalp or skin condition-related. Medically, it is regarded as a non-inflammatory form of dermatitis that manifests in scalp scaling. It affects both males and females, and it is not restricted to a particular region or climate. For its treatment, shampoo is recommended, and there are different brands specifically for males and females. Ringworm is another fungal infection that appears in a circular rash that is red and itchy. Ringworm is caused by parasites that live on the cells in the outer layer of the skin; it is spread through human-to-human contact with infected skin. Ringworm is a common infection among young boys in the rural areas of sub-Saharan Africa, and this may not be unconnected to hygiene and malnourishment factors. Ringworm is treated with antifungal creams or lotions. Equally, eczema is a condition that causes dry, itchy, cracked, rough and inflamed skin, and it can happen to humans at any age. Research has further shown that it can occur as a result of allergies. Eczema can be treated with anti-itchy cream or anti-itchy medication. In spite of the availability of different medical cures for these dermatological diseases, many people in sub-Saharan Africa adopt the use of automobile brake oil to treat them. In this case, brake oil is applied to the infected part of the scalp or skin. In some cases, the surface of the infected part is scraped and brake oil is applied, and the method can be crude and painful.

vii. **Beef Cooking:** The use of certain brands of lime soda or soft drink to cook meat, especially beef, to soften meat is becoming rampant and popular in in-home and commercial cooking. Thus, the purchase or consumption of certain brands of lime soda goes beyond thirst quenching and socialisation among the consumers because others have 'invented' a new usage for the soda drink. The prevalence of the 'act' is popular among commercial caterers who cook in large quantities for parties and other social events, and this may not be unconnected to the need to get many things done within a short time regardless of the implication on consumers' health. In the same vein, painkiller brands with paracetamol (also known as acetaminophen or para-hydroxyacetanilide) formulation or composition are equally being used for meat cooking to quickly soften it, like lime soda drinks.

viii. **The Case of a Lip Balm Brand:** The case of a lip balm brand that is made from aloe vera is another heart rendering incidence of product exaggeration in the market. Originally, the lip balm was meant to be used during the harmattan season to help with dry and parched lips, but consumers in the northern part of Nigeria contrarily use the product to treat piles.

The fact is that the issue of product exaggeration and stigmatisation comes in different shapes than the examples stated earlier, and it varies in different economies and among consumers across the African markets.

The Cruz

In the work of Lou et al. (2021), the issue of product exaggeration is described as excessive reputation, which has effects on the authenticity of information dissemination from the recipients' angles and perspectives. In other words, information presented in the public forum is subtly, deliberately or consciously embellished in order to make users patronise or continue usage of such products in many other ways outside of formal or conventional usage. According to Joseph Ajah, a Lagos-based independent marketing communications consultant, product exaggeration is not officially acknowledged; it arises from consumers' experimentation or accidental discovery. By implication, while the consumers inadvertently use the product for seemingly wrong purposes, the marketers or organisations make fortunes from such exaggerated claims in terms of sales and revenue thereof. Product exaggeration can be formal or informal; formal, when it is encouraged and presented, and perpetuated by the organisation concerned through the different marketing communication media. For instance, a firm's salesmen, in their bids to convince and persuade buyers, exaggerate the performance, function and benefits of products. And advertisements and other media are equally used to achieve the same exaggerated claims. Dife Adebiyi, head of product development at Bluebird Communication, corroborates that it is not ruled out that firms could engage in product exaggeration, but it is never outright mentioned. Product exaggeration leads to arousal in consumer interests in products and, in many instances, leads to product abuse. However, when it is consistently applied, the backlash can be more damaging to products and organisations' images. For instance, it makes consumers feel unreal, reduces consumers' perception of product image and affects consumers' evaluation of the medium or celebrity used for marketing communication (Lou et al., 2021). The informal exaggeration happens when it unofficially emanates from a corner of a market by consumers through the accidental discovery of unofficial usage of products, and it spreads through word of mouth. Invariably, these developments affect the willingness to patronise and the continual use of such brands.

Varsha et al. (2019) (Goffman, 1963, cited in Varsha et al., 2019, p. 28) describe product stigmatisation as a phenomenon that degrades, differentiates and discredits the lives of individuals and groups. Naturally, the concept is used for human beings; however, the application to products is imminent to accentuate the negativity and wrong perception ascribed to certain brands without official information either from producers or from industry regulators. Largely, stigmatisation attaches inferiority and negativity to brands, and this generates negative emotions on the part of consumers. By and large, it reduces demand for brands, and, in many cases, consumers feel restrained and inhibited from consuming such products in public. Unfortunately, the wrong perception and negativity generated may deny consumers real value or benefits that may improve wellness, livelihood and general satisfaction.

The question always arises as to whether marketing communication has a way of correcting the incidence of product exaggeration and stigmatisation. The experts' opinions reveal that correcting such market developments may be easy, complicated and dicey, depending on the depth of exaggeration and stigmatisation. According to Dife, when a product or service is stigmatised, advertisements can be used to correct such notions, and even sometimes reputable professionals and influencers can be used to correct the stigma and reinforce its benefits and uses. On the other hand, Ajah asserts that in Nigeria

> every consumer product requires and receives approval from regulators of that product category before it is sold to consumers. Any attempt to respond to consumer perception by communicating this new consumer-determined extended use, will be very difficult because it would most likely require new vetting and approval from the regulator of the new category. It may also require new product registrations and new vetting guidelines.

This may largely contribute to many organisations' seeming or deliberate silence on exaggeration and stigmatisation that affect their brands.

To a large extent, unabated product exaggeration and stigmatisation may affect the efficacy of marketing communication because the perceived new usage or negativity might have a deep-rooted stronghold on consumers. Ajah believes that product exaggeration or stigmatisation may not impact marketing communications for the affected brands unless it is established that the extended use is damaging the reputation and integrity of the brand in question. In such an event, the brand owner would most likely develop a communication strategy that reinforces the brand essence and, if necessary, repudiates the negative perception attached to the extended use. In the same vein, Dife asserts,

> stigmatization to a large extent sometimes drowns out whatever marketing communication efforts that's made on products and services. So, when such an issue arises more critical and creative efforts are considered to help correct the notion e.g., inviting a neutral party to give reviews on product, professional opinions that are respected, press statements, trials and unbiased reviews by influencers.

The imminent question in society is always: Where are the regulators with the increasing incidence of product exaggeration and stigmatisation? The belief is that the ubiquitous presence of APCON/ARCON and NBC should have checked the developments and reduced them to the barest minimum. APCON, which is now known as ARCON, works to determine if an advertisement is worthy of broadcast, and equally ensures that the benefits communicated are true and that the contents of the advertisement are not offensive for public consumption. Before a product is approved for marketing communication, samples are taken for testing and try-out, and the outcome determines the approval for such a product. This helps the regulatory agency stay abreast of the information being disseminated to the consuming public. On the part of NBC, it monitors the marketing communication that can be offensive to the general public, especially where such communication escapes the eagle eyes of ARCON, and the media station used is penalised. By and large, the regulatory agencies seemingly do not have control over and check on what happens in the market after product and communication contents have been scrutinised and approved for marketing communication. According to Dife, regulatory agencies may carry out investigations on brands if such exaggeration or stigmatisation causes uproar in society. Dr. Hezekiah Ajagbe, a director with Allianz Media, further hinges on the roles of the regulators as the bodies that have the responsibilities of ensuring communication of products and brands. Languages are within the scope of sane and moderate appeal to avoid claims that cannot be substantiated or that may impinge on the emotion of a particular target audience.

To conclude that the twin challenges of poverty and illiteracy that are prevalent in developing countries may contribute to the thriving of product exaggeration and stigmatisation may be difficult. However, communication experts believe that the propensity to get more for value among certain segments of the population cannot be ruled out. Ajah asserts,

> It is rational to expect that poor and illiterate members of the society will be more disposed to experimenting with products beyond their intended and stated use, with a view to stretching the benefits accruable from a single purchase. That way, they may believe that they could save themselves some valuable money.'

This is further corroborated by Mide Campbell of Etu Odi Communication Ltd., who says that consumer low exposure and illiteracy have a correlation with poverty, and this makes product exaggeration thrive, which in turn creates opportunistic sales. Mide Campbell further asserts that marketing communication has a greater role to play in reducing, if not eliminating, product exaggeration and stigmatisation. In a twist to the argument, Ajagbe of Allianz Media stresses that though poverty may account for such behavioural patterns on the part of consumers,

> However, the major factor is lack of proper education on the part of the source of this product exaggeration and by extension the stigmatisation. Most brands/products owners just want to market their products and when the level

of information at the disposal of the creative shop is inadequate, they could develop the communications that may be offensive and without recourse to standards and control and will eventually exaggerate either the potential or efficacy of the said product, and these are very common with health products.

Questions

1. Do you think the regulatory agency and organisations have done enough to check and reduce the incidence of product exaggeration and stigmatisation in developing countries like Nigeria?
2. What would have made an organisation close its eyes to the aftermath of stigmatisation and exaggeration in spite of the long-run effects on organisations' performance, and how can this be corrected?

References

Lou, H., Cheng, S., Zhou, W., Yu, S. & Lin, X. (2021). A study on the impact of linguistic persuasive styles on the sales volume of live streaming products in social E-commerce environment, mathematics. *Basel*, 9(13), pp. 1–21.

Varsha, J., Amrita, B. & Tarishi, M. (2019). Digital storytelling as a solution to destigmatise products: Case of women lingerie from India. *Journal of Business and Management*, 25(1), pp. 25–48.

World Bank's Global Economic Prospect (2018). Available at: https://thedocs.worldbank.org/en/doc/575011512062621151-0050022017/original/GlobalEconomicProspectsJan-2018SubSaharanAfricaanalysis.pdf

World Bank's Global Economic Prospects (2022). Available at: https://thedocs.worldbank.org/en/doc/18ad707266f7740bced755498ae0307a-0350012022/related/Global-Economic-Prospects-June-2022-Regional-Highlights-SSA.pdf

World Bank Group Publication (2015). *Africa's population boom: Will it mean disaster or economic and human development gains?* Available at: https://www.worldbank.org/en/region/afr/publication/africas-demographic-transition

www.statista.com https://www.statista.com/statistics/1120999/gdp-of-african-countries-by-country/

Contributors

Joseph Ajah has over 20 years of experience working in marketing communications. He is skilled in advertising, event management, public relations and stakeholder relations. Joseph is versatile. He is an editor and actor. He has worked on a rich portfolio of brands in Nigeria and Ghana, including Standard Chartered Bank, Tigo, Globeleq Africa, UBA, and Etisalat, among others. Joseph (B.A. (Hons.) English Studies; Executive MBA (Marketing)) facilitates presentation skills, crisis management and spokespersons' training.

Adedife Adebiyi, MBA, and an alumnus of BMA (Brand Management Academy), is a highly experienced multiskilled brand manager and growth lead with a proven track record of orchestrating successful strategies to drive operational excellence and sustainable growth. With almost a decade of adeptly navigating complex communication campaigns and business environments across Africa, she has built a reputation as a trusted advisor when it comes to communications in Africa and is currently serving as the business development manager at Bluebird Communications. Her expertise includes the deployment of ground-breaking campaigns that leave impactful footprints, identifying opportunities and connecting brands to their audience through the use of thought-provoking strategies.

Dr. Hezekiah B. Ajagbe is equipped with a sound academic background and a wealth of experience in advertising, spanning mainstream advertising, experiential marketing and marketing communications. He has strong strategic planning skills that have been made available in leading pitches across the mainstream advertising agencies where he worked, with over 20 years of experience in the business trade of positioning brands for positive perception and top-of-mind. Hezekiah is an innovation enthusiast and early adopter of technology, often interested in jumping into innovations that help to improve performance in the sub-sector where he finds himself. He is an astute academic with a passion for impacting knowledge in marketing. He is a part-time lecturer at the prestigious University of Lagos Business School. His wealth of experience is being brought to bear on the Allianz Media business to draft the transition strategy of the business into the digital space.

Dr. Hezekiah had his first and second degrees from the prestigious University of Ibadan and his doctorate from the Atlantic International University, the United States. He is multilingual and has vast experience in the West African economy. He had his secondary education in Ghana and can speak their language fluently. During his experience in the advertising industry, he has worked with LTC-JWT Advertising, SO&U, Fuel Communications, Exp Nigeria and digital out-of-home advertising agencies. He is a deep thinker and an astute businessman.

Olumide Campbell is essentially a strategic thinker, whether it is positioning a brand to exploit market opportunities, designing a route-to-market for a new product/startup or planning a sales promotion. He cut his teeth in strategy as a management consultant, and before joining Etu Odi, he had headed the Strategic Planning Unit and Multi-National Business Unit, respectively, in JWT Nigeria.

With over 22 years of experience crafting business and brand strategies for companies in various markets and life cycles, Olumide has worked across industries (FCMG, FSI, ICT, Agro-allied and services) to offer best-in-class management and brand marketing services.

Olumide is an avid film critic and is currently working on a few stories to help project the African Renaissance. He loves to teach, travel and watch movies and is involved in training in a professional capacity.

2 Know Your Mate

The Psychographic Side of Beer Consumption in Nigeria

Ayodele C. Oniku, Omotola Elatuyi and Oluwaseun O. Otayemi

Introduction

One common word that has a functional role and cuts across all Nigerian languages and tribal differences is *Owambe*. The average reveller knows the meaning, the social power and the social implication of it in Nigeria; even foreigners
who are ready to mingle and key into the country's social circle know the full
effects of the social language. One thing that any stranger or a first-time visitor in
Nigeria will find amusing, entertaining and impressive is the different manners of
socialisation, be it in a beer parlour, clubhouse, guest house or ubiquitous weekend
party popularly called *Owambe*. In all the appellations or social names that it may
be called, be it fun-making, partying or revelling, it all points to one fact: social
enjoyment.

The social entertainment is popular among the Yoruba tribe, who are believed to
be the creators and foremost organisers of such party. It also connotes merry-making
and communal celebration, is a much-looked-for activity where old and new
friends catch up, there is opportunity to see long-lost/distant family relatives, and
more importantly, there is the food and drink largesse that comes with the occasion
and some bit of affluence to show off. Owanbe is also prevalent across tribes in the
East and North when Kinsmen gather to celebrate.

Pointedly, any avenue to socialise is never wasted among Nigerians; it is cher-
ished and made effusive with all passions and networking. From time immemorial,
the opportunity has always been created to socialise and party, and this is manifested in the different celebrations that take place in Nigeria. For instance, a baby
christening, especially a firstborn, is an opportunity to bring people from all walks
of life together to felicitate with the new parents, but beyond this is the huge planning behind the party to commemorate the occasion. Likewise, marriage, funeral,
birthday, housewarming, knighting or chieftaincy installation, new car etc. So, it is
a culture that every new acquisition must be celebrated and a party must be initi-
ated. What does the celebration entail? There must be food, drinks, music, chairs
and tables, and the quality, variety and depth of the entertainment are a function of
the host's pocket size.

It is not uncommon to attend a party, say a birthday, wedding, funeral, knighting etc., and all sorts of assorted foods are provided free for the guests, and it can

DOI: 10.4324/9781003441274-3

be extended to extra takeaways for guests to relish the party at home. Likewise, different alcoholic and non-alcoholic beverages are provided for the enjoyment of guests. Thus, champagne, whisky, wine, lager beer and all other drinks are provided, which gives guests the liberty to make choices for their satisfaction. It is a common trend to see either guests or hosts make comparisons of parties based on the benchmarks of quality and varieties of foods, drinks, takeaways and manners of entertainment to show superiority.

The Case of Lager Beer

Presently, Nigeria has over five full operational breweries producing different brands of lager beer, including a few international brands being produced under licenses from the parent companies. Notable among the breweries in the country are Guinness Plc, Nigerian Breweries Plc and International Breweries Plc. In the past few years, the industry has witnessed different merger and acquisition deals that consolidate the industry into three major breweries in the name of the aforementioned breweries. The development was largely prompted by the entrance of SAAB Miller into the Nigerian market and the new deal between Nigerian Breweries and Heineken International.

Guinness Plc

Guinness Plc made entry into the Nigerian market in 1962 and became the first Guinness brewery outside Europe (the United Kingdom and Ireland). The brewery produces the popular Guinness brands in Nigeria, and in recent times, it has increased the number of brands in its stable to cover beer brands. In other words, Guinness Plc has diversified into lager beer with brands like Guinness beer, Harp, *Orijin* and *Satzenbrau*. Harp brand happens to be the company's oldest lager beer to compete with the other lager brands in the industry, while the company maintained a monopoly position in the stout market until recently, when those competing brewers introduced their brands of stout drinks. The Harp Lager brand used to be the flagship of Guinness Plc, which was first brewed in Nigeria in 1974. Harp was the toast of revellers and ubiquitous in all parties, clubhouses and beer parlours, competing with Star and Guilder lager brands. Its popular slogan remains memorable with many revellers and lager consumers: 'Harp for Happiness.' Harp ranked among the leaders in the industry in its first 40 years in the Nigerian market. Satzenbrau lager beer was somehow short-lived in its market dominance, and this may be attributed to both internal factors of strategy failure and industry competition. The speculation was that it was introduced to the Nigerian market to rival Nigerian Breweries' Guilder brand, which was a strong competitor in the market from the 1990s until the 2000s.

Today, *Orijin* has become Guinness Plc's flagship brand in the beer category, and its innovative brewing might be attributed to its herbal contents in that it is sourced from the local ingredients of African herbs and fruits. *Orijin* lager beer is of two varieties in the market: *Orijin* Bitters and Origin Zero. There is also *Orijin*

Spirit in the category of spirit and whisky. Orijin has its target, and to a large extent, it is doing well because of its positioning as a beer and herbal drink, which endears it to many consumers.

Nigerian Breweries (NB) Plc

Nigerian Breweries Plc has been the pioneer brewery in Nigeria since 1949. The company was incorporated in 1946, and rolled out its first product, Star Lager Beer, in 1949 and the company has been waxing stronger since that time. Over the years, the company has deepened its operations vertically and horizontally in the Nigerian market. For instance, the lager category has grown from the Star brand to include Gulder, More, Lite Star, Star Radler, 33, Goldberg, Life, Tiger and Heineken brands. The stout category covers Legend Extra Stout, Turbo King and Williams Dark Ale, and the company equally specialises in a few brands in the non-alcoholic category.

In recent times, the Star brand has been extended to include Star Radler, which comes in red fruits and citrus varieties, and Star Lite. Both varieties of Star Radler have a lesser alcoholic content of 2%, while Start Lite is a normal lager beer. Star has undergone rebranding and repositioning on many occasions, and these have kept the brand strong in the market since 1949. To different generations, Star Lager beer represents different relishing and socialising brands, and the recent association of Radler varieties with feminine personalities is giving socialite women and revellers a voice in the social circle. Gulder is one of the two premium brews of 100% barley in NB Plc's stable. 'The Ultimate,' as it was known in the 1990s until recently, is a class on its own associated with the 'Big Boys' and consumers who want to show class in lager consumption. The earlier respect it commanded in the market was its distinct bottle design, which separated it from other lager green bottles that are the same irrespective of brewers. Symbolically, many consumers read certain positive and implicit meanings in the design, which gives it a distinct class. The second premium brew is Heineken, which is an international brand. Heineken was first introduced into the Nigerian market in the 1960s and later re-introduced in the 2000s after a long disappearance in the market. Its international brand quality is giving NB Plc a vintage place among international brands that were once dominated by Guinness Stout. Today, international brand is a strategic pursuit in the industry to meet the needs of certain consumers who prefer global brands and premium brews, and this is one of the hedges Heineken enjoys today.

International Brewery (IB) Plc

International Brewery was established in 1978 in the ancient city of Ilesha in Osun State. The flagship brand that heralded IB Plc into the world of lager brewing is Trophy Lager Beer. The brand grew from local patronage to a national brand and is currently enjoying international acceptance, thanks to Nigerians in the diaspora. The recent international merger of the company with SABMiller/AB InBev and local acquisition and merger with breweries in the country, to a great extent, changed the operational landmarks of the company to become one of the major players in the Nigerian market. The company has increased the lager line in addition to Trophy to include brands like Hero, Eagle, Castle Lite and Budweiser, an international brand that the company leverages to compete in the global brand market. One of the numerous advantages that merger and acquisition affords the organisation is the strategic location of the different breweries to compete effectively in each region, and this IB has achieved with Hero Lager in the south-east of Nigeria and Trophy Lager in the south-west. The company stout category comprises the Trophy Stout and Eagle Stout brands.

Nigerian Revellers' Idiosyncrasies

The need to capture the inherent factors that underpin many consumers' consumption behaviours is very strategic in the beer industry, while the predominant factors might be refreshment, socialisation and pleasure; however, these factors have different interpretations and manifestations for many consumers. While the organisations might rely on segmentation to target the right consumers for product acceptance, hence patronage, there is certain pertinence in the marketplace that the eagle eyes of strategists may not have captured.

The Love Nest

Age-long tradition does not allow women to drink, especially publicly, in many cultures in Nigeria, and this is a sort of restriction on women's beer and other alcohol consumption, until recently with the millennial under the new social move of 'Girls' Night Out.' The exception is where it serves medicinal purposes. Yet, many women have unconsciously used lager brands to rate the social status and potential of men they associate with in social circles. Many of these women don't drink or are light drinkers, but they are versed in and understand the social language of beer quality and brand rating. Joy, a 28-year-old student, testified that it is a common denominator in her circle to date and socialise with men who drink the right brands, and the rightness of a brand is measured in the premium brew, retail price and brand popularity among men with deep pockets. Sade, a single mother in her mid-thirties, corroborates that there are brands that are socially classified as brands for 'unskilled labourers,' and it will undermine her social status to sit with men who drink such brands. She furthers that in local parlance, such brands are called 'Bricklayers' Beer,' and the reason for the appellation is that she and people in her social circle believe the brands are not premium brewed and relatively cheaper. She does not drink beer but believes that the beer brand speaks volumes about a man's calibre and social status. Stella frankly said that she would swap tables in any social gathering if her man sat on the table filled with 'Bricklayers' Beers' brands. She further said that she has witnessed on many occasions where men who subscribe to the status rating of beer would speedily turn the available brand into an empty cup and dispose of the bottle because it would be difficult to know the particular brand in a cup. This scenario always plays out where the 'Big Boys' brands are not available at parties or have been sold out in clubhouses or beer parlours.

Invariably, behavioural patterns may have multiple-dimensional effects in the market, especially in the way organisational approaches strategy formulation. For instance, it is highly plausible that many men's choice of beer brand is influenced by networking factors. In other words, the propensity to be in the right circle for business networking and social relevance may influence many people to change brand loyalty from 'Bricklayers' Beer' to 'Big Boys' brands. Equally, the need to please and achieve opposite-sex attraction may influence the choice of beer brands or change in brand loyalty. This has strategic implications for organisations in deeply understanding why consumers choose beer brands outside the conventional segmentation practice.

The Table Gazers

It is not uncommon in any party or social gathering to see a table filled with different types of beer, assorted wines and brandy bottles; likewise, non-alcoholic drinks like fruit juice, soda and other sorts, and this goes to imply that the table you sit on determines the attention you receive in a party. Hence, many revellers and socialites carefully choose the tables at which they sit at a party, club or other social gathering. For instance, a table at a party filled with fruit juice, bottled water and fruit wine is a pointer to the fact that such a table will be occupied by religious people whose tenets and doctrines rule out alcohol consumption. An alcoholic or beer drinker at such a table may not experience full enjoyment and satisfaction at a party. On the contrary, a party's table filled with alcoholic drinks like beer, wine, whisky and brandy is meant for different consumers who relish alcohol.

Deeply, a table filled with alcoholic drinks has categories, which in Nigerian parlance are VVIP (Very, Very Important Personality) table, VIP (Very Important Personality) table and popular table. Thus, it is not strange to hear table arrangements being designated in these manners; though not official, the social subconsciousness of revellers and attendees projects it. What makes differences across the table is the category of drinks arrayed on the table, and individual social status dictates the table reserved for him/her. However, some revellers and socialites choose the table to sit at because it determines the treatment and level of enjoyment or satisfaction received at a party, club or social gathering. Thus, merely looking around a party venue or any social gathering, many consumers choose a table that fits their social equity, where they can afford to pay for the drinks they choose, where they can meet up with the social qualifications or where they can meet up with the Joneses. By and large, these consumption behaviours are underpinned by the ratings ascribed to each lager beer, which means some brands fit into VVIP choice, VIP choice and popular choice.

The question remains: Do brewers know this, and to what extent does it reflect in marketing strategies, positioning, marketing communication and pricing? Ladi, a university student, shared his behaviour: As a student, I know my level and the brand I can afford, which has been my loyal brand. However, I won't miss every opportunity to go to a club or attend a social gathering with my uncle, who is a bank manager. Such has always been an opportunity to have a 'Big Boys' experience' with premium brew and mingling with men and women in the middle and upper middle class of Nigerian business and corporate circles.

Psychologically, every table gazer has a social status to maintain, and this entrenches his pattern of beer consumption. He consumes beer and chooses a brand that is socially and societally accepted to meet a particular social appellation or circle that he or she dreams of or pursues to fit into, and anything less may amount to dissatisfaction. Even when he consumes a brand that he deems socially inferior to his or her dream, it is a temporary or intermittent consumption. To them, a brand of beer is a dream to pursue and an enjoyable way to entrench or establish social status.

The Signature

The main attribute and peculiarity of the signature are anchored on leveraging the established rank, rating or image that each beer brand commands to project an individual social image. In other words, revellers and socialites anchor their social image on a lager brand reputation in social circles to affirm their social status. In other words, revellers and socialites or, in Nigerian parlance, '*the Happening Guys*' leverage the established social image and revelling reputation of a beer brand to establish a social image and acceptance for themselves in a social circle. Thus, it is not strange to hear names or appellations like 'Gulder *(gooder)* Man' for someone who drinks the brand Gulder Lager to project his social status; 'Shine, Shine Bobo' for a consumer who builds loyalty with Star Lager to entrench his social relevance and image; and '*Odeku Baba*' for someone who drinks nothing less than Big Guinness Stout (the 75 cl bottle) to prove his social worth in a social circle.

Inherently, the signature exhibits a strong nature of affinity in their consumption based on the social status and social relevance they desire to achieve and project. The category of consumers through public outings shows a sort of compulsive desire for the brand, and no other brand can give such relish and satisfaction in terms of taste, social relevance and image. Equally, the signatures' decision is not fixated on conspicuous consumption because the behaviour cuts across all the brands, be it premium brews that are normally more expensive than other brands or brews. Each signature displays loyalty in their choice because the brand's accepted image fits into consumers' existing or intended social image.

The Villagers

The psychography of the villagers is that they are strong beer consumers, but the choice of brand is based on the locational factor in that they show affinity and loyalty to brands produced in their localities, which can be their towns, their state of origin or the region of the country they come from. It is a common saying among the Yoruba, especially the Ijesha people and Oshun State indigenes, to hear '*Tiwa n Tiwa*' interpreted as '*Let's celebrate or embrace our own.*' It is a local language term standing as solidarity for consuming Trophy Lager beer. Likewise, the Igbo people from the eastern part of the country, especially the indigenes of Anambra State, claim loyalty to Hero Lager beer on the terms '*Turu ugo lota*' meaning '*Our pride has come back*' or '*Nkea bu Nke Anyi*' meaning '*This is our own.*' The unanimous resolution is based on economic, employment and going concern factors to make sure the organisations remain operational and profitable because it creates employment in the communities or regions, and equally brings development to the community or state. On a larger scale, the Villagers believe that their committed patronage is a sign of loyalty to the community and a way to pledge support for the continuity of the breweries' operations. In other words, their patronage is another way to express their innermost feeling that the success of the breweries is also the community's success, and the failure of the breweries is a failure of the community. So, everything will be done in their capacity through patronage to see to the going concerns of the organisations.

Any Justification?

The issue and debate in the industry are to what extent brewers' strategies should recognise these special segments in the industry. The segments look invisible, silent and less powerful to the brewers, but they are sizeable, recognisable and strategic to the beer parlour owners, clubhouses and *Owambe* organisers, and they determine their orders and internal operations classification of customers, or segmentation in a nutshell.

For instance, it is a daily experience among beer parlour owners to have customers who have an allegiance or loyalty to certain brands, and they keep such customers by always reserving the brands for them because they know the behaviour pattern is: '*Nothing but my brand.*' Madam Chi, the owner of Chi Beer Parlour, recounts her experience with some customers; she said there is a set of middle-class businessmen customers, and when they visit on their regular days of the week, she does not need to ask for their preferences because it has been a permanent order for them, and all she does is serve them. She furthers that among these categories are the signature who use their brands to project social image. According to her, anytime Chief comes around, he will just say '*1759*,' which is another name to order Guinness Stout among loyal consumers, and Chief will not accept any bottle less than the 660-ml bottle popularly called '*Odeku.*' In one of her experiences with Chief, on this day she sold out all the 660-ml bottles before Chief arrived, and to her surprise, Chief refused to take the 450-ml or any other smaller size of Guinness Stout as a replacement. Chief was so angry on this fateful day that he left Chi Beer Parlour without any order. She confessed that she never allowed such an event to happen again, and another day it would have happened. She quickly ran to another beer parlour to buy for Chief. She said the Chief chose *Odeku* as his signature, and his case is one of the most extreme cases of the signature's behaviours that happen in the business. On asking her why she needs to accommodate such customers, she emphasised that such customers are predictable, regular consumers, and they make forecasting easy for her, and importantly, they form sizeable orders in the business. For instance, Chief would visit five times a week with a minimum order of two bottles of 660 ml per night.

Deluxe Lounge's Manager shared his business experience with customers; according to him, on a regular basis, some groups of customers who hail from the same town or state come around to socialise; equally, some come to hold their community meeting in the lounge; and one peculiar buying pattern is that a large number, if not all, would demand the brand that the brewery is located in the community, state or region they come from. He furthered that on many occasions, he has witnessed extreme patronage where customers would refuse brands even though the brewer is situated in their present locations but insisted on brands brewed in their home state, community or region they hail from. For instance, certain customers from the Ilesha axis, Ijesha environs or Oshun State, even among the Yoruba customers, may insist on Trophy Lager beer and refuse Hero Lager beer, even though both brands are brewed by the same company, International Brewery Plc., and vice versa for certain customers from Anambra State or the eastern part of Nigeria. To these customers, patronage is not about the brewer's brand's quality or taste; it is about identification with brands from their place of origin and community.

It is claimed among industry experts that most of the breweries in the industry are beginning to recognise what consumers are looking for, hence shaping a lot of the marketing campaigns, including the branding. There is a need for a better understanding of the beer consumer's effects and demand. These changes in demand play a vital role in future sectoral dynamics, as depicted earlier. Beer drinkers are increasingly seeking new tastes, experiencing different consumption situations and food matching, and demonstrating a willingness to pay for superior-quality products. Moreover, consumption situations and occasions continue to be relevant segmentation variables. Based on the different segments discussed earlier, each of them represents a different ambience that is suggestive of their lifestyle. Today's consumers have more choices, more information and higher expectations than ever for their varied tastes and preferences and would remain true to their choices.

Therefore, recognising this set of customers in marketing strategies, especially in communication, distribution policy and pricing strategies, helps to maintain brand loyalty and equity. The corollary of this is that many village people wait until when they see their brand in consumer beer; likewise, many signatures travel for their brands; the Love Nest uses available communication to choose their brands; and the table gazers are driven by the positioning strategies of brewers for their brands.

Question

As a consultant and marketing strategist, what will be your recommendations for maximising the potential of these salient consumers for brewers?

3   One-Stop-Shop

A New Marketing Strategy in Recreational Business in Jos, Plateau State: A Case Study of *Vei-So-Nshi Bar*

Kennedy O. Nwagwu, Robinson A. Bananda and Cornelius N. Wukari

Introduction

The hospitality industry is an important aspect of the dynamics of every economy, but it is of particular significance to its tourism sector as it is what provides services like refreshment, entertainment and lodgings to stakeholders. They also provide employment and pay taxes in addition to being direct players in the retailing of products from breweries and non-alcoholic beverage sectors (Adesope et al., 2023). The industry is made up of four subgroups, namely food and beverage; travel and tourism; entertainment and recreation; and lodging (EHL Insights, 2023). The industry is therefore described as a diverse assemblage of businesses that provide leisure services to their markets (Denomme & Shin, 2021). In specific terms, the industry is populated by hotels, motels, guesthouses, restaurants, airlines, resorts, bars, hospitals, nightclubs, pubs, zoos and a vast array of other like-minded businesses out there (Spacey, 2023).

Plateau State, the Europe of West Africa, is rich in cultural heritage, with impressive natural resources, clement weather with an abundance of sunshine, waterfalls and volcanic/inspiring rock formations. The mountain vegetation of the Jos Plateau and the variety of its handicrafts culminated in its attractive scenic beauty, like none other in Nigeria. Jos, its capital city, is identified in Nigeria's National tourism master plan as a hub for the central scenic cluster. Added to its picturesque beauty, McKenna (2023) notes that Plateau people are friendly and 'welcoming people.'

The foregoing has no doubt contributed to the development of hospitality businesses in the state, particularly in the state's capital city of Jos and its environs. But even at that, it has been shown that most communities, especially those outside of the city centres, have less access to quality recreational facilities within easy reach (Wapwera et al., 2023). This is where businesses like Vei So Nshi Bar come in to service those gaps by providing several recreational services at the same place. As of the last count, there is hardly any other brand that does what Vei So Nshi Bar offers within a radius of 10–20 km.

One-Stop-Shop as a Marketing Strategy to Outwit Competition

As its name suggests, Vei So Nshi Bar is a bar, but as a matter of deliberate marketing strategy, it is a one-stop shop that provides a wide range of recreational and

DOI: 10.4324/9781003441274-4

relaxation services. To achieve this, Vei So Nshi Bar houses such businesses as a nightclub, restaurant, fast food, sports viewing centre, roasted fish/beef centre (i.e. steakhouse) and a tea house. Though still in its early stages having been in business only for about three years, Vei-So-Nshi Bar has gradually acquired the status of an important institution in its sphere of operation by becoming a source of entertainment for a vast number of leisure seekers. Sitting on an ideal atrium of a major road, it is within easy reach of a large swath of towns, suburbs and villages that have become its source of a continuous flow of clientele. Please see some illustrative images in the Appendix.

The name 'Vei-So-Nshi,' which in the native Berom language means 'Come let's commune together' resonates so much with the local communities and has gained brand-wide acceptance. With this acceptance, Vei-So-Nshi Bar has come to mean 'the place to be.' As noted earlier, this bar brand provides services like a free viewing centre to her sports and football-loving customers in a cosy and relaxing setting. And then fast foods like shawarma and ice cream, which appeal especially to the female and younger segments, are available. While the nightclub scene is mostly non-existent in a large swath of its immediate communities due to a combination of security concerns and poor purchasing power of the people, Vei So Nshi Bar has been able to provide some semblance of that recreational activity by its use of visiting DJs at weekends and its state-of-the-art musical equipment that plays nonstop music for its customers to dance to without payment of gate fees. This has resulted in a brand that is yet to be replicated by any competitor, hence the vibrant patronage the business has continued to enjoy. At weekends, their services are usually oversubscribed, and most times management has to embark on crowd control and sometimes turn back people to avoid overcrowding.

Application of Marketing Tools by Vei So Nshi Bar

While marketing is made up of several diverse concepts, each of which is equally important to the success of every organisation, this study has investigated the application of the 7Ps of marketing (namely Price, Product, Promotion, Place, People, Processes and Physical evidence) as practised by Vei So Nshi Bar. Questions that bothered mainly those seven tenets of marketing were asked of the managers of the business as a way of throwing more light on their practical application by businesses in the recreational sector of Nigeria.

Product: To ensure good and quality service delivery to customers, Vei So Nshi Bar makes sure that customers are served in a proper manner and with hygienic and unadulterated products in sparkling and clean utensils. Also, customers are served promptly by clean, courteous, polite and neatly dressed staff. For quality control, a system is put in place to monitor food preparation to prevent contamination. It is important to note that management ensures that defective products are replaced at no cost to the customer.

Management provides a variety of products and services. Home deliveries and space/hall rentals for meetings, birthday parties and events are also available. Though Vei So Nshi Bar's business model allows these other businesses like the restaurant, steakhouse and fast food to run independently, they all must conform to policies and standards as set by management.

Pricing: In the area of pricing, the firm adopts a variety of pricing techniques such as cost-plus pricing, comparative pricing and penetration pricing, especially for new products. However, on some products, the firm sells based on prices recommended by third-party suppliers.

For easy transactions, management allows both cash and non-cash payment options. The use of point-of-sale terminals, automated teller machines, and transfers is prevalent. Selling on credit is usually prohibited except on rare occasions and for big-time and loyal customers.

Promotion: For promotion, Vei So Nshi Bar hardly relies on traditional promotion media such as television, radio, newspaper or billboards; rather, they make use of such media as electronic signs, posters/signposts, handbills (flyers) and branded clothing. There is no dedicated social media handle; however, employees privately promote the firm on Facebook and WhatsApp. Sales promotion is a popular promotional mix element deployed at Vei So Nshi Bar. Price discounts, buy one get one free (BOGOF), sweepstakes (raffle draws) and rebates are often used to boost sales.

Place: The location of the business was a deliberate strategic choice anchored on the following considerations: Proximity to a major road that connects several high-population centres; closeness to several residential neighbourhoods yet distant enough to ensure minimal noise pollution to neighbours, adequate space, which is large enough for car parking and buildings, and, in consideration of security, the firm's location is close to a military camp. In addition, extra security is provided to protect customers and their cars.

Process: At Vei So Nshi Bar, the business is organised to ensure efficiency and delight for the customers. As a result, both space and setting up of the various service points are done to ensure a short turnaround time. Customers are promptly attended to. Also, at pay points, customers are not delayed. The system at the firm ensures a good working relationship with suppliers to ensure all needed materials are always available. The same is true with the maintenance units, as they ensure that there are no issues with refrigeration, lighting or space management, especially during live shows. There are systems in place to detect and dislodge troublemakers, all for crowd control, especially at weekends.

People: To be competitive and satisfy their customers, Vei So Nshi Bar understands the role of a motivated, honest and competent workforce. To ensure these criteria are met, the journey starts at the recruitment stage, where management strives to ensure that people with the requisite experience and passion are recruited. Usually, background security checks are done before recruitment. Recruits are trained on proper and acceptable conduct. The firm provides accommodation for staff. Conflicts are resolved quickly. According to the manager, 'We operate as a family so staff are encouraged to open up their minds and proffer suggestions.'

To enhance productivity and ethical conduct, the firm offers one of the best pay packages in the sector; salaries are promptly paid and there are regular staff awards, incentives and bonuses based on profit achievement at the end of the year.

Physical Evidence: This refers to the environment in which the service is delivered, including those cues that customers look out for as evidence of the quality of the service since they cannot examine the service before they can consume it. In the case of Vei So Nshi Bar, the cosy and warm environment, spiced with a full of ornamental plants and flowers added to clean restrooms with an abundant water supply comparable to any top-class hotel around, assures guests of value for money. The presence of open halls guarantees guests a free flow of fresh air. The VIP huts and the light music provide the right ambience that puts this brand ahead of the competition.

Conclusion

This study presented a detailed analysis of the application of modern marketing concepts, particularly the 7Ps of the marketing mix among home-grown businesses. This informed the choice of Vei So Nshi Bar, a business that chose to be unique in its ways by offering services that are over and above the norm. In carrying out this case study research, we conducted interviews with the managers, physically studied their processes, looked out for pieces of evidence to see if they were indeed resonating with their target market, and arrived at the conclusion that the business is adequately applying the concepts of marketing in its operations.

Figure 3.1 'The Interior Sections of Vei-So-Nshi Bar.'

Figure 3.2 'The Interior Sections of Vei-So-Nshi Bar.'

Figure 3.3 'The Interior Sections of Vei-So-Nshi Bar.'

References

Adesope, A. A., Obadimu, O. O., Oguntoye, T. O., Oyewo, I. O. & Olusesi, O. E. (2023). Determinants of hotel patronage and challenges in Oyo State, Nigeria. *KIU Journal of Social Sciences*, 9(2), pp. 29–33. Kampala International University ISSN: 2413–9580.

Denomme, S. & Shin. (2021). *Hospitality Industry*. Available at: Study.com

EHL. (2023). *Hospitality Industry: All Your Questions Answered*. Available at: https://hospitalityinsights,ehl.edu

McKenna, A. (2023). Plateau state Nigeria. *Encyclopedia Britannica*. Available at: https//:www.britannica.com.

Spacey, J. (2023). *45 Types of Hospitality Industry*. Available at: https//:simplica.com

Wapwera, S. D., Namo, J. A., Azi, M. B., Timlok, W. T., Shehu, P., Bulus, J. A. & Shwargak, G. J. (2023). The impact of recreational facilities on residents of Jos North LGA. *Bokkos Journal of Science Report (B-JASREP)*, 2(2), pp. 13–29. https://jasrep.org/index.php/jasrep. https://doi.org/10.47452/bjasrep.v2i2.6013

Part 2

Consumer Behaviour and Young Consumer Behaviours

4   Condom Use and Acceptance

A Case of Nigerian Society

Ayodele C. Oniku

The popular phrase 'Who gets This Rain Coat' in the mid-1980s heralded the re-introduction and a new phase of condom usage and acceptance in Nigerian society, courtesy of SFH (Society for Family Health), which pioneered the new social marketing strategy for condom usage and acceptance in Nigeria. SFH was a non-governmental organisation (NGO) founded in 1983 and incorporated in 1985 by the trio of Prof. Olikoye Ransome-Kuti, Mallam Dahiru Wali and Hon. Justice Ifeyinwa Nzeako, who were Nigerians, and Mr. Phil Harvey. From its inception, the focus of the NGO was to effect positive changes in behaviours towards major common health challenges in Nigeria, like the prevention and treatment of malaria, HIV/ TB treatment and prevention, reproductive health family planning. The NGO's operations covered other West African countries like Ghana, Sierra Leone and Liberia.

In 1994, the NGO embarked on a campaign to influence positive behaviour towards condom acceptance and usage among the citizens; hence the social marketing strategy with the theme: 'Who gets this Rain Coat?' The event was followed by the distribution of the Gold Circle brand of condoms in states like Lagos, Ogun and Oyo, and this was later scaled up to cover other parts of the Nigerian Federation. The organisation enjoyed the support of other international organisations like USAID and the UK's Department for International Development. By 1997, the company was distributing 17 million condoms, and by 2009, the NGO was distributing over 200 million condoms at subsidised prices annually across Nigeria.

Simultaneously, there was a sponsored project in Nigeria focused on condom acceptance in the country. The essence of the survey exercise was to unravel and correct wrong impressions about condom usage among Nigerians, which has generated consumer resistance and rejection, and, most importantly to encourage its usage. The need for contraception was found to be important to reduce and curtail the population explosion that was imminent in Africa. Nigeria was significantly involved in the project because of the high rate of annual population, especially among the illiterate, the less-educated and religious people.

However, before the survey in the 1980s, the condom was not strange to people in sub-Saharan Africa. It was known and regarded as a male-focused contraceptive, which used to make it more of a 'male thing' in that every discussion, acceptance and usage were more or less viewed from a male perspective, and it was residual to men of the house. Beyond the fact that condoms are male-focused, other factors

DOI: 10.4324/9781003441274-6

contributed to their unpopularity among the people of Nigeria before the survey exercise. Largely, culture contributed to its seemingly early rejection among the people based on the following reasons:

- It used to be a culture of contraceptives among Europeans, not Africans.
- Many religious bodies like Islam, Christianity and African Traditional Religion's (ATR's) messages didn't encourage contraceptives; in fact, in many instances, contraceptive usage was categorised as the sin of murder.
- African culture largely supported large families because children are 'gifts from God.'
- Thriving fables and the unfounded assertion that condoms can slip into a woman's virginal and a condom could melt, hence leading to the death of women.
- Only used in brothels and offered by prostitutes to their clients.
- Condoms and other contraceptives are for educated people who are undermining the African culture of large families etc.

Beyond the culture-related factors, there are other beliefs and insinuations associated with condoms that affect rejection among women as well.

- Contused usage of condoms for a long time could cause prolonged menstruation and much blood loss.
- The condom may not allow women to discharge during intercourse.
- The condom may rupture and affect women's chances of pregnancy.
- A condom can get contaminated, hence leading to HIV infection.
- Condoms are susceptible to leakage and tear during intercourse.

The New Beginning

The new acceptance of condoms emerged in the early 1990s, when the perception changed among married couples based on the belief that with condoms, you could enjoy sex with nursing mothers. Hitherto, the belief, which still thrives in some tribes, that sex with nursing mothers could make semen affect the quality of breast milk and cause babies to fall sick and even die (Renne, 1993), and this was the era when mothers breastfed for a long time, like one year or more, and children spacing ran into two to three years. Thus, many couples found solace in condoms to enjoy intimacy during lactation. This new belief, hence the acceptance of condoms, resulted in the prevention of early pregnancy and longer lactation. In Renne's (1993) study, it was revealed that many men accepted and used condoms for intimacy with wives three months after delivery and continued at least once a month for the next nine months during lactation.

The work of Atchison et al. (2019) further expounds on the acceptance of contraception in all shapes and forms in selected countries in sub-Saharan Africa, which includes Nigeria, and the findings show a high improvement in acceptance based on improved knowledge of the benefits; erosion in misconception about contraception and improvement in self-efficacy among married women and men.

The wide spread of AIDS in the 1990s also made condoms accepted among many people because they became the cheapest and readily available preventive means for HIV infection. So, men and women who engaged in casual sex or were in doubt about their partners accepted condoms for prevention purposes along-side other STDs. Coincidentally, the fear of AIDS infection alerted many sexually active people to embrace condoms, and the objective overrode every other fable or culture-related factor associated with condom resistance and rejection.

The New Face

Forty years later, the state of condom acceptance and usage is being revisited to determine the extent of the efficacy of the survey exercise and research study and the SFH and other NGOs' efforts in Nigeria. Thus, in 2020, AHF (AIDS Health-care) in Nigeria carried out a survey titled 'Condom Accessibility and Use in Nige-ria.' The focus of the study is aimed at 'increasing awareness on the use of condoms as a contraceptive and for safer sex.' The exercise revisits the perceptions and dis-positions of Nigerians across ages, religions and tribes towards condom usage and consumption. On a larger scale, the new survey exercise reveals robust information that points to the current trends in condom acceptance and reception among the citizens, which to a large extent shows how cultural factors, male dominance and feminine fears of the past have been reduced or eliminated in twentieth-century condom consumption among Nigerians.

The statistical information reveals the following:

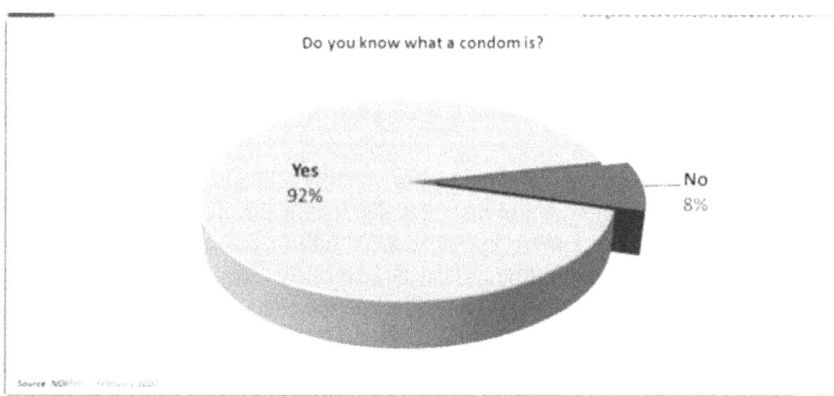

Figure 4.1 Do you know what a condom is?

The graph in Figure 4.1 reveals that 92% of the population agreed with the question that they knew about the use of condoms. This has clearly shown an improvement in the awareness of condoms compared to the study of Renne (1993), which revealed that a larger percentage knew condoms as Durex (the brand name for condoms produced by a British firm). Impliedly, the brand name

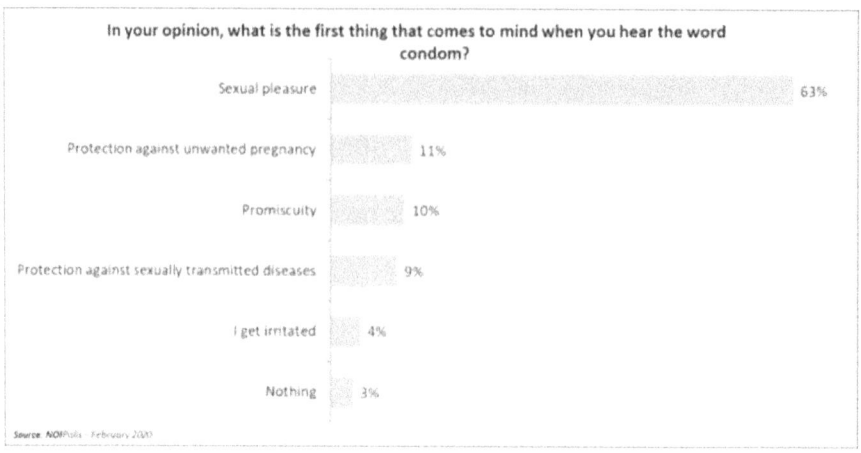

Figure 4.2 In your opinion, what is the first thing that comes to mind when you hear the word condom?

Durex was wrongly used as a generic name for condoms, which may affect brand recognition and awareness across the brands in the market. It could also be ascertained that the use and popularity of condoms are no longer limited to married couples but include all categories of sexually active individuals. The development may also allude to a change in women's purchase decisions regarding condoms in the market, whereby women buy male condoms for use with their partners.

Equally, to different people, condom usage and acceptability amount to different objectives and purposes. To some, it is a means of sexual fun and pleasure in that using a condom gives them the pleasure and confidence they desire, be it in married couples or in any other type of relationship. Another category chooses a condom to avoid unwanted pregnancy because they see it as a sure form of contraception in any relationship, be it a marriage or a casual affair. Another category of users are consumers who largely indulge in casual and other forms of extramarital relationships, and the reasons behind the preference for condoms are protection from venereal diseases, deadly AIDS/HIV and unwanted pregnancy. Invariably, the promiscuous category may be associated with people who engage in casual relationships, where there is no commitment in relationships, especially with commercial sex workers. The other category believes in condoms as sure protection against diseases; in other words, the only reason for condom consumption is for protection against any sort of venereal disease.

The last categories of consumers have nothing to do with condoms based on irritation and 'not a choice,' and these consumers might be found among the religious people who hold staunchly to religious tenets, people who are faithful in relationships, and people who believe that condoms as contraceptives will not give them the sexual pleasure they desire and are against family planning. And the other

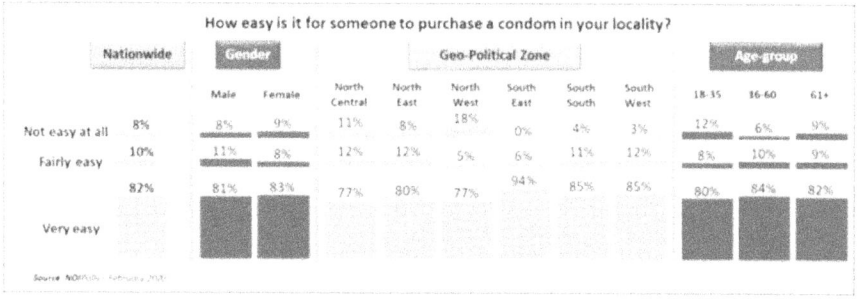

Figure 4.3 How easy is it for someone to purchase a condom in your locality?

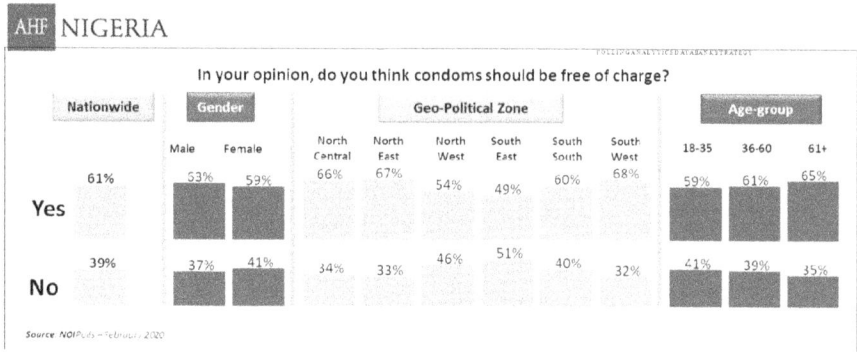

Figure 4.4 In your opinion, do you think condoms should be free of charge?

consumers in these categories are the 'risk-takers' who indulge in promiscuity and casual sex and yet don't use condoms for protection.

The ease of getting condoms from local pharmacies has improved over time based on the graph in Figure 4.3, and this may be attributed to improved marketing communication and knowledge of the health benefits and significance of condoms. From the graph, there is an improvement in its availability and ease of purchase across all variables used to measure it.

iv

The popular opinion that condoms should be made available for free may not be disconnected from the traditional behaviour of the government to give free items to the citizenry when it comes to popular programmes like child education, adult education, vaccination against polio, and other health and social programmes of the government. From the previous programmes, such programmes are made available free to encourage new attitudes and behaviours among the citizenry.

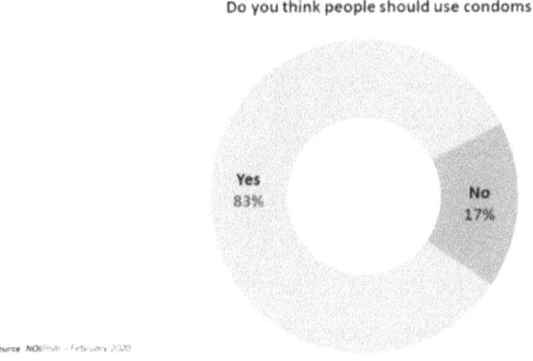

Figure 4.5 Do you think people should use condoms?

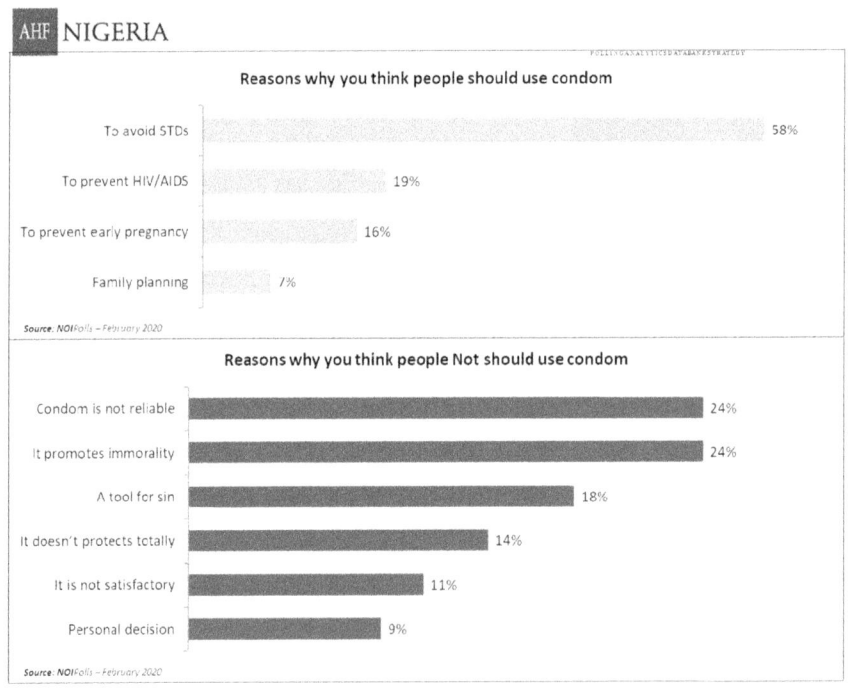

Figure 4.6 Reasons why you think people should and should not use condoms.

v

The response that condoms, like other contraception, should be used and encouraged among people is a clear clarion call to curtail the widespread use of HIV/AIDS and other STDs, birth control and prevention of unwanted pregnancies etc. This is a result of increasing awareness of the benefits inherent in condom usage.

vi

The ranking of reasons why condoms should be used reveals the importance attached to condoms among the citizenry; for instance, the prevention of STDs and HIV/AIDS is paramount among the people above family planning. This is a pointer to decision makers on the perception of people and users of contraception, and this may call for more robust public awareness of its function for family planning and prevention of unwanted pregnancy.

Equally, the mindset of the people that condoms are not reliable and that they promote promiscuity needs to be addressed to correct certain opinions and beliefs that could become a stronghold among certain people, especially non-users.

vii

The response shows that a larger percentage of people have not embraced or adopted condoms for their functions, and the prevalence is higher among females, in the North East and North West, and among the older generation.

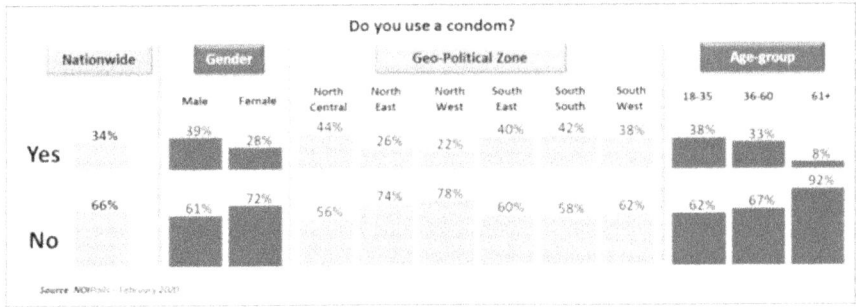

Figure 4.7 Do you use a condom?

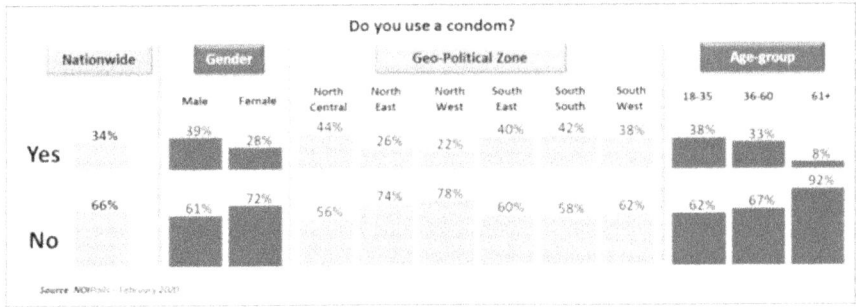

Figure 4.8 Personal reasons for using a condom.

viii

The plots reveal the different reasons for the adoption and usage of condoms across the different regions of the country, and potentially the reasons vary, which could be a source of information for government and health agencies' policy formulation. Many reasons can be alluded for the different responses and findings. The fear of misconceptions around condom use may be responsible for many women's resistance and rejection in family planning and the prevention of unwanted pregnancy, as well as the belief that women believe in a larger family than men in African society. On the other hand, women might be well-disposed to condom use when the issue of STDs and AIDS/HIV comes into consideration; could it be the issue of trust in relationships or guard against any eventuality in extramarital affairs that may lead to regret?

ix

From the responses above, religious doctrines and tenets play the strongest reason for the rejection and non-adoption of condoms among the citizens, and this is also a potential area for marketing communication and government and health agencies' policies. Creating a balance between religious tenets and doctrines and economic reality in maintaining a family is a choice among people in the absence of any legislation on the number of children a family should have. Unilaterally, many couples or consumers have chosen religious doctrines and tenets on the premise that 'Children are gifts from God' above the economic capability to maintain a family, and the choice is not based on the level of education, tribe or social exposure but solely on religious indoctrination. On the other hand, there are pastors, imams and other religious title holders who reflect on the economic reality and capability to define the size of family; they embrace condoms

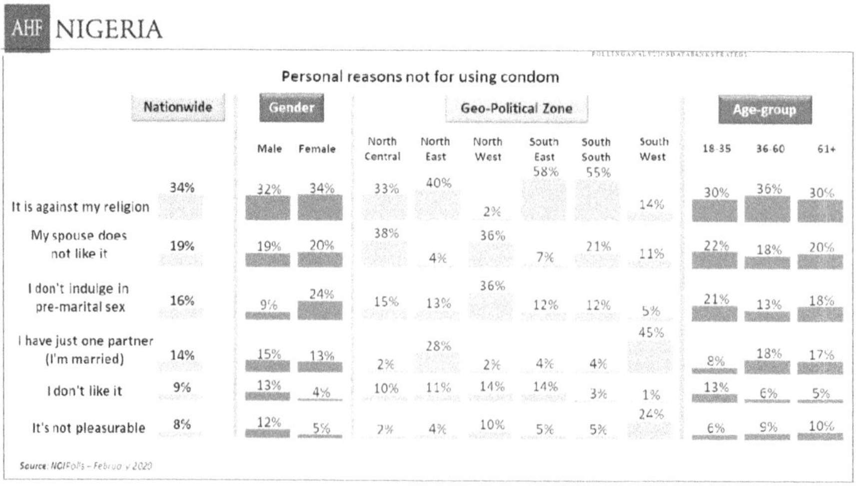

AHF NIGERIA

Personal reasons not for using condom	Nationwide	Gender		Geo-Political Zone						Age-group		
		Male	Female	North Central	North East	North West	South East	South South	South West	18-35	36-60	61+
It is against my religion	34%	32%	34%	33%	40%		58%	55%	14%	30%	36%	30%
My spouse does not like it	19%	19%	20%	38%		36%	2%	7%	21%	11%	22%	18%	20%
I don't indulge in pre-marital sex	16%	9%	24%	15%	13%	36%	12%	12%	5%	21%	13%	18%
I have just one partner (I'm married)	14%	15%	13%	2%	28%	2%	4%	4%	45%	8%	18%	17%
I don't like it	9%	13%	4%	10%	11%	14%	14%	3%	1%	13%	6%	5%
It's not pleasurable	8%	12%	5%	2%	4%	10%	5%	5%	24%	6%	9%	10%

Source: NCIFoPS – February 2020

Figure 4.9 Personal reasons not for using a condom.

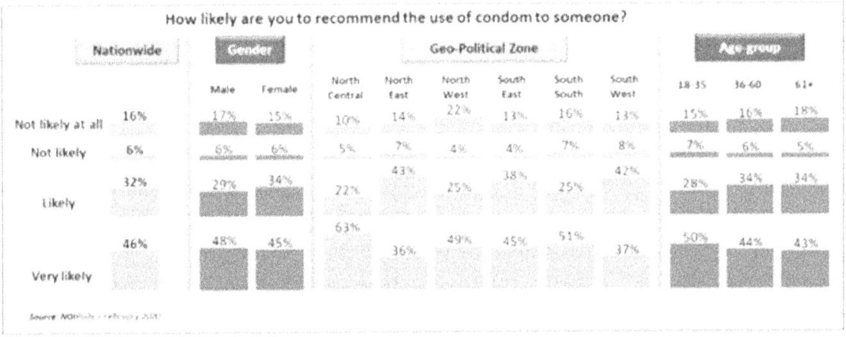

Figure 4.10 How likely are you to recommend the use of condoms to someone?

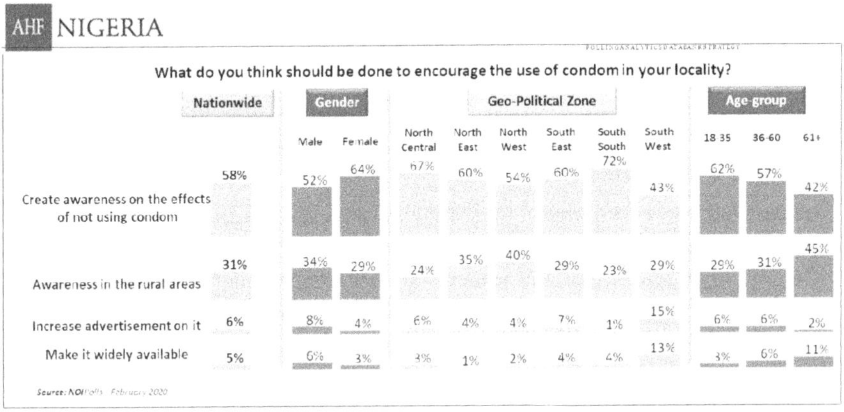

Figure 4.11 What do you think should be done to encourage the use of condoms in your locality?

and other contraceptives to adhere to the personal goal of a small family. The ATR believers might do well in maintaining a small family, but they are largely enthusiasts of polygamy; invariably, acceptance of condoms and other contraceptives is selective in maintaining a relationship and the number of children with each wife.

x

The response above reveals the likelihood of existing users (male and female) to recommend condom usage to other adults for different reasons ranging from prevention of STDs, HIV/AIDS, unwanted pregnancies and family planning.

xi

The need to create more awareness of the effects of not using condoms is strongly supported and approved in the study by the citizenry. This is further followed by the need to improve awareness creation about the benefits and consequences of not using it in rural areas of the country.

Will Marketing Communication Continue the Wonder?

The role of marketing communication cannot be overemphasised in attitude formation and attitude change among users of products, especially where a product or service is faced with resistance or rejection among consumers. The strategies have worked in many instances in government awareness creation for health and educational programmes. For instance, it took consistent and aggressive marketing communication for the Nigerian government to achieve the present success level in polio eradication, child vaccination for other preventable diseases like measles, tetanus and rubella, and the entrenchment of female education and child education in some parts of the country. The 2020 UNAIDS report on 'Developing Effective Condom Programmes' shows its 'The condom programme pathway – a theory of change' which has three layers of operations: Condom Program Stewardship, Condom Program Development, and Condom Program Outcome. The Condom Program Stewardship (pp. 7–8) stresses different activities that are commercial and marketing communication-oriented, and the programme covers, among others:

- Leadership and coordination that stretch across all sectors engaged in condom programming (public, NGOs and commercial).
- Community engagement and leadership: Full engagement of communities and organisations representing people at higher risk and key populations in planning, resource allocation, implementation and oversight of condom programming.
- Production and dissemination of programme analytics to inform intervention design and monitor progress.

Thus, integration of the programme stewardship with marketing communication tools may go a long way in attitude formation and change in condom use and adoption.

Reports have shown that the use of marketing communication has increased to a greater extent given the present success rate in condom use and adoption in Nigeria. In an interview with a top executive of one of the distributing companies in Nigeria with Premium Times, Dimos Sakellaridis of DKT International Nigeria, he stressed that education is very important in its usage and benefits, and the organisation implements it through different marketing tools like advertisement and social media platforms.

Another organisation that is involved in condom use awareness in Nigeria is the KISS (Keep It Safe and Sweet) organisation, which has employed what it calls the Total Marketing Approach (TMA) in its operation to make condoms a popular product for safe sex and healthy sexual life. According to the company's policy on TMA, it embarks on demand-generation activities using social media marketing to reach youths and adolescents with a 'correct and consistent condom use message.' The organisation further seeks a collaborative effort with the National Agency for

Food and Drug Administration and Control (NAFDAC), a government agency involved in food and drug regulations, to ensure that only government-registered condoms are in circulation.

While corporate organisations, NGOs and the government believe they have substantially invested in condom awareness in Nigeria and are looking forward to a safer and healthier sex life among Nigerians and a profitable market, the imminent question remains: Will the tribal and cultural sentiments in some parts of the Northern region not invalidate the hope? Also, will the rising religious bias among certain sects and affiliations against condom use and adoption as contraception is not a clog in the wheel of progress to achieve condom benefits? Equally, have advocacy groups lost their effectiveness in the market compared to their effectiveness in the 1980s up to the 1990s?

The Place of Distribution

To complement the expected attitudinal change that may result from aggressive communication, experts are pushing forward the inevitable roles and imminence of effective distribution policies and strategies in the whole setting. The question remains: With the peculiarity of the health sector, what distribution policies, models or frameworks will be appropriate to accommodate the ethnic, tribal and religious differences that prevail in the Nigerian market? Also, serious consideration needs to be given to the rural areas where most of the resistance and low use are occurring.

According to the report, there is still a 600 million condom demand gap in Nigeria (Premium Times, 2021); this is a business opportunity for an organisation that knows its onion when it comes to distribution management. One of the critical issues raised is that the market is bedevilled with market inefficiencies, which seriously hampered access to condoms and equitable and sustainable availability to the most vulnerable populations (NOI polls). According to the study sponsored by AHF and NACA, 'the outpouring of free condoms and inadequate targeting of fee condom distribution' has contributed a lot to the distribution inefficiency in that the practice disrupted sales of commercial and socially marketed condom brands. The question remains: Is the free condom crusade antithetical to effective demand generation and creating the wrong attitudinal behaviour to purchase among a section of consumers?

A school of thought has also advised on using non-pharmaceutical commercial outlets like motor parks, hotels and brothels, as well as open shops in public places like tertiary institutions and retailers. The proposition was faulted on the ground that such practice has caused the invasion of the Nigerian space with non-NAFDAC-accredited brands in the market because unscrupulous importers see an opportunity to bring different brands whose qualities cannot be ascertained into the Nigerian market.

On the other hand, if the market experts and the regulatory body insist on pharmaceutical retailing outlets and other health institutions like hospitals, health centres and the 'Chemist Shops' etc., will these outlets provide effective retailing functions, and will they achieve expected market coverage distribution as seen in convenience products and retailers' functions?

Questions

1. Are there roles for marketing communication approaches to arrest the rising negative attitude towards condom use among adults, adolescents and married couples?
2. Develop a marketing approach to counter tribal and cultural sentiments against condom use in a section of the country.
3. From the statistics, despite the crucial roles of women in condom use and adoption, their consent is very low in the graph. Will advocacy groups be strategic, or what is the communication strategy?
4. Develop a strategy that shows the complementarity of market communication and distribution to fill and close the demand gap.

References

Atchison, C. J., Cresswell, J. A., Kapiga, S., Nsanya, M. K., Crawford, E. E., Mussa, M., Bottomley, C., Hargreaves, J. R., & Doyle, A. M. (2019). Sexuality, fertility and family planning characteristics of married women aged 15 to 19 years in Ethiopia, Nigeria and Tanzania: A comparative analysis of cross-sectional data. *Reproductive Health*, 16(6), pp. 1–14.

How to Close Nigeria's 600 Million Condom Demand Gap – February 13, 2021. Available at: www.premiumtimesng.com

Premium Times. (2021). World Contraception Day: Nigerians Should Carry Condoms like Sanitary Pads, Shaving Sticks (Interview) – September 26, 2021. Available at: www.premiumtimesng.com

Renne, E. P. (1993). Condom use and the popular press in Nigeria. *Health Transition Review*, 3(1), pp. 41–56.

UNAIDS. (2020). Developing effective condom programmes. *Joint United Nations Programme on HIV/AIDS*.

Contributor

Abimbola Owolabi Bowoto is a native of the Ilaje Local Government Area of Ondo State, Nigeria. He is a pharmacist with sales and marketing experience in pharmaceuticals and social marketing organisations spanning over a decade. He started his sales and marketing experiences as a medical representative and grew through the ranks to become a sales and marketing specialist in pharmaceuticals as well as non-governmental organisations using a social marketing approach on the need for the use of condoms and reproductive health. He is a strategic thinker and analytical in his approach.

Importantly, Mr. Bowoto was instrumental to access to the Survey Report on Condom Accessibility & Use in Nigeria (February, 2020) that informed the study. The Survey Report was prepared and produced by AIDS Healthcare Foundation (AHF), Nigeria – NOI Polls.

5   Sustainable Shopping Mall Visit

The Case Study of Young Saudi Shoppers

Ibrahim A. A. AlZahrani, Saheed A. Gbadegeshin, Zainurin B. Dahari and Rachid Moustaquim

Why Shopping Mall?

The act of shopping is an important facet of consumers' lives and the activity is constantly evolving, making the investigation and understanding of this field an important effort. While the mall industry appears to be saturated in many of the developed western countries, it is now witnessing fast growth in Saudi Arabia through the flow of both local and foreign investments. In fact, some of the world's largest shopping developers are now in the Middle East, which has been noticed in the last five years. For instance, Majid Al Futtaim, which operates several shopping malls in the region, is set to invest up to SR20 billion by 2029 in Saudi Arabia's entertainment and retail sectors. This also includes the construction of a 300,000-square metre mall in the capital city, Riyadh, called the Mall of Saudi Arabia. One of the motivating factors for this trend could be the rise in disposable income of young Saudis because there are more young men and women joining the workforce in Saudi Arabia than before. The increase stimulates the consumption or demand for more goods. To buttress this, a Saudi Arabian newspaper popularly known as Saudi Gazette published in 2018 that the total value of the kingdom's retailing industry would grow from $106 billion in 2018 to $119 billion in 2023. Of this, the newspaper stated that offline retailing values would see a $10 billion increase, from $103 billion in 2018 to $113 billion in 2023. Its estimation seems to be right because the recent increase in the number of tourists in the country, especially early this year, shows that the retailing industry of the Kingdom is growing rapidly. Also, it is mentioned by an organisation called Global Media Insight in 2022 that the Saudi Arabian population is seeing a tremendous surge in the number of newly opened shopping malls in the hopes of catering to the needs of its emerging consumer market.

Why Sustainability?

Recently, Mollenkamp (2023) explained the philosophy of sustainability, how it works and its benefits, and even gave examples. He states that the basic meaning of sustainability is an effort to ensure that a specific process is maintained for a long period of time while the environmental, social and economic aspects of it

DOI: 10.4324/9781003441274-7

are not derailed. This author states further that the philosophy of sustainability is to ensure that all resources are not wasted so that future generations can enjoy them. He elucidates that when sustainability is considered in any process operation, its operations would be futuristic, financially considerate and mostly important, and environmentally and societally beneficial. Considering Mollenkamp's (2023) explanations, it can be agreed that it is reasonable to examine how shopping malls are sustainable because they are capital-intensive businesses. For instance, building a shopping mall would cost hundreds of millions in any currency, such as euros, dollars and SR.

Why Young Saudis?

It was said sometimes ago by Jones (2003) that Middle Eastern consumers from affluent oil-based economies love to shop. This motivated Belwal and Belwal (2014) to mention that it is imperative for retailers to understand their consumers' shopping motives and their effects on patterns of consumption. It is even important for Saudi Arabia, which has multi-ethnic and multi-country consumers, local customs and customer expectations. According to Amine and Tanfous (2012), store preferences in the Islamic world demand special attention as consumers might have either a resistance towards the format or a foreign image, indicating congruency between some western values and the values of the local Arab-Muslim culture. Also, it is a challenge for mall managers to create a feasible competitive marketing strategy that is not easily duplicated by competitors.

Furthermore, the Global Media Insight states that about 45% of the population is under 25 years old. Hence, the shopping demand to satisfy the needs and wants of this segment is rapidly increasing. However, shopping and mall visits are not usually determined by ordinary behaviour. The scholars, such as Shim and Maggs (2005) and Hartman et al. (2006), affirmed that mall visitation has proximal determinants, like motives, attitudes and beliefs. Unlike motivation, values are culturally determined.

Apart from the aforementioned reasons and motives for shopping, some studies, including Sohail (2009), Kulviwat et al. (2009) and Zhou and Li (2010), argue that the majority of case studies of shopping malls and the motives for mall visits are mainly derived from a Western context. Thus, it is unclear whether similar factors and patterns in which the Western world would influence mall shopping behaviour will be found in an Arab context. This is an important issue since researchers have not highlighted if there are fundamental differences between developed nations and developing nations on issues such as business environment and consumer behaviour.

Additionally, values that predict shopping mall behaviour of western shoppers may be different from the ones that predict Arab shoppers' behaviour, given their sharp differences in cultural backgrounds. Moreover, although there is substantial research on shopping motives and shopper typologies based on shopping motivation, only a few studies have been published in a non-western context, according to recent studies such as Chang and Yeh (2016) and Pare and Pourazad (2017). Likewise, the majority of existing studies focused on adult shoppers, whereas young people also have purchasing power.

Considering the above factors, it seems interesting to know the motives and attitude of young Saudis when visiting shopping malls since a mall image reflects the total value of a shopping centre, which can be a competitive advantage that is difficult for competitors to duplicate. It is also interesting to analyse their shopping motivations so that the retailers can influence the consumption behaviour of this specific group. Likewise, it is interesting to provide knowledge, challenges and opportunities for marketing professionals about the young Saudis because they represent the majority of the population.

How the Motives Were Found?

To gather the necessary information, a qualitative research method was decided to be used. Specifically, a structured brief interview was used so that the collected data could be systematically analysed. Young mall shoppers in Riyadh, Saudi Arabia, were contacted at one of the biggest malls. Riyadh was selected because it is the most populated city in Saudi Arabia. Additionally, Riyadh has the highest number of shopping malls compared to other cities in the Kingdom. The interview is made up of three sections. The first section focused on demographic data so that relevant respondents could be identified. This section focused on age and education. The second section focused on their shopping habits, especially their shopping frequency and average time spent during a mall visit. The last section concentrated on shopping orientations. Altogether, the data of 100 young people were considered for this case study.

What Are the Motives?

With respect to frequency of visits, the majority of interviewees visit a shopping mall once a month. This was then followed by the interviewees, who visit a shopping mall once every two weeks, then once a week. As for the number of different shopping malls visited in the past two weeks, most shoppers said that they did not visit any malls. This was then followed by those who said that they went to one to three malls. Regarding the exact shopping mall visited by the interviewees, it was discovered that the most visited malls, as stated by the interviewees, is Nakheel Mall. Panorama Mall was the next regular visited mall among respondents, while the least visited mall was Al Qasr Mall.

Also, about the average time spent in shopping malls, the majority of the young shoppers spent 30 minutes to an hour in malls, while the remaining (30%) claimed that they spent an hour and a half to four hours in malls. With respect to the number of different stores visited, it was found that a significant number of young shoppers visited between one and five malls (about 84%), about 14% visited between six and ten malls, and only 2% visited more than ten malls.

As for the part of their salary spent in malls, about 50% of young shoppers spent 5% or less, about 37% spent between six and 20%, and 13% of them spent more than 20% of their monthly expenditures in malls. This means that 50% of males spent 6% or more of their monthly salary when visiting malls.

Most importantly, when they were asked about the main motive for visiting shopping malls, they responded that they were attracted by the interior design as well as the internal atmosphere of shopping malls. They emphasised that they preferred the aesthetic and exploration of the mall. They also mentioned that they do not visit malls solely to avoid unpleasant experiences and to keep themselves occupied. Most of them also said that they visit shopping malls to find interesting products or new products. These young shoppers were clear that they do not visit shopping malls to cope with stress, avoid traffic congestion and relieve boredom.

What Are the Implications of these Motives to Saudi Arabia and Foreign Business People?

Not only that the young Saudi shoppers are mall-goers; this study shows that this segment is willing to spend a significant amount of their monthly expenditure in shopping malls. Hence, mall managers should take this opportunity to improve certain aspects of their offerings in order to attract this segment. Firstly, mall executives are expected to place emphasise on interior designs. For example, they could adjust the ambience of the malls to foster a foreign feel to the shopping experience. Next, they could use shopping malls as a place to launch or showcase new products since young shoppers are highly receptive to new experiences and products.

Also, the mall managers should provide a place for them to socialise. This could be achieved by adding the latest trending restaurants and entertainment shops to the tenant mix. Finally, they are advised to address the environmental and social concerns of a growing segment of customers anxious about sustainability, especially on issues relating to sustainable space, organic products, fair trade, low-emission product choices or carbon-efficient, water- and energy-efficient and local-made products.

Another important thing to state is that the Islamic law that only allows men to do shopping and that the women should be accompanied by men is now abolished. This means that young women are now able to enter shopping malls freely. Thus, this implies that the motives and attitudes of young Saudis might be different in the future. Also, the country is now open to international tourism due to the Vision 2030 anchored by the Crown Prince of the Kingdom, which has business implications for young people's attitudes towards shopping mall visitation.

What Are the Questions or Lessons for Business Students?

As a business student, this case reveals key issues associated with consumer behaviour. You are required to think and provide answers to the following questions:

a) What do you understand about the money value of the shopping mall industry in Saudi Arabia?
b) What do you understand about the young Saudi shoppers' behaviour?
c) Why are young Saudi shoppers an important potential market for businesses or retailers nowadays?

d) Do you consider the shopping mall business a sustainable business in Saudi Arabia?

e) What do you think about Vision 2030 for shopping malls in the country?

f) What can you learn from the findings of this case in terms of marketing strategies?

g) Assuming that you were a part of the case study consortium, what would you have done differently?

Providing answers to the aforementioned questions enables you to have an overview of shopping mall behaviour, which is becoming an important phenomenon in today's business environment in the Middle East countries.

As far as we know, the business environment is no longer stable. Therefore, the use of case study to understand the shopper's behaviour would help to prepare your future minds for exploring and preparing business opportunities and strategies.

References

Amine, A. & Tanfous, F. H. B. (2012). Exploring consumers' opposition motives to the modern retailing format in the Tunisian market. *International Journal of Retail and Distribution Management*, 40(7), pp. 510–527.

Belwal, R. & Belwal, S. (2014). Hypermarkets in Oman: A study of consumers' shopping preferences. *International Journal of Retail and Distribution Management*, 42(8), pp. 717–732.

Chang, T. & Yeh, H. (2016). Gender differences in Taiwan's hypermarkets: Investigating shopping times and product categories. *Asia Pacific Journal of Marketing and Logistics*, 28(4), pp. 650–662.

Global Media Insight. (2022). *Saudi Arabia Population*. Available at: https://www.globalmediainsight.com/blog/saudi-arabia-population-statistics/ (Accessed on 1 May 2023).

Hartman, J. B., Shim, S., Barber, B. & O'Brien, M. (2006). Adolescents' utilitarian and hedonic web-consumption behaviour: Hierarchical influence of personal values and innovativeness. *Psychology and Marketing*, 23(10), pp. 813–839.

Jones, G. (2003). Middle East expansion – The case of Debenhams. *International Journal of Retail and Distribution Management*, 31(7), pp. 359–364.

Kulviwat, S., Bruner, G. & Al-Shuridah, O. (2009). The role of social influence on adoption of high-tech innovations: The moderating effect of public/private consumption. *Journal of Business Research*, 62(7), pp. 706–712.

Mollenkamp, D. T. (2023). *What is Sustainability? How Sustainabilities Work, Benefits, and Example*. Available at: https://www.investopedia.com/terms/s/sustainability.asp (Accessed on 1 May 2023).

Pare, V. & Pourazad, N. (2017). The big bazaar: An examination of Indian shopping mall behaviour and demographic differences. *Asia Pacific Journal of Marketing and Logistics*, 29(5), pp. 1160–1177.

Saudi Gazette. (2018). *Saudi Arabia's $106bn retail industry forecast to grow 12.3% by 2023*. Available at: http://saudigazette.com.sa/article/550005

Shim, S. & Maggs, J. (2005). A cognitive and behavioral hierarchical decision-making model of college students' alcohol consumption. *Psychology and Marketing*, 22(8), pp. 649–668.

Sohail, M. S. (2009). Marketing strategy, related factors and performance of firms across Saudi Arabia. *Journal of International Business and Entrepreneurship Development*, 4(4), pp. 286–301.

Zhou, K. & Li, C. (2010). How strategic orientations influence the building of dynamic capability in emerging economies. *Journal of Business Research*, 63(3), pp. 222–224.

6 Storytelling

Coke and the Alpha Generation's Demand Behaviours

Ayodele C. Oniku and Olamide Akintimehin

Introduction

Coca-Cola is the leading bottler of sparkling and non-sparkling beverages in the world, though the organisation operates under different names in different nations based on the licensing agreements and licensees' corporate names. For instance, in Nigeria, it operates under the name Nigeria Bottling Company Plc. Coca-Cola has its headquarters in Atlanta, Georgia, USA, and the organisation owns, licenses and markets more than 500 non-alcoholic beverage brands across the world, of which the Coke brand is the flagship, the most popular, and is made available in all markets. The organisation that started operation in 1886 in the United States has a presence in more than 200 countries, and the net operating revenue as of 2009 is $37.3 billion.

Coca-Cola's operation in Africa is over 90 years, and precisely 70 years in Nigeria in 2022. The organisation has grown by leaps and bounds, from the importation of finished products to the construction of plants across the 54 countries on the continent. In 2017, the President of Coca-Cola West Africa, Peter Njonjo, said in his interview with Bloomberg that $600 million would be spent on its new products by 2020 in Nigeria and $17 billion in Africa. The success of Coca-Cola in Africa, like in other parts of the world, cannot be disconnected from the adoption of intensive and equally entertaining commercials and other marketing communication tools. The earlier commercials on the continent were on the radio, posters and billboards before the television's advertisements started; equally, the earlier advertisements were largely foreign with little or no African content.

Storytelling as a Marketing Communication Tool

Storytelling is the art of relaying tales to an audience, sometimes with added flair and drama. In general, storytelling can be used for amusement, instruction, entertainment, historical record-keeping and moral instruction. It has increasingly become a potential tool in marketing communication because of certain inherent advantages it possesses. For instance, it can readily and effectively serve to remind and convince in business commercials because of the storylines that underpin it and the capacity to make formal information informal for an audience's entertainment.

DOI: 10.4324/9781003441274-8

Tabassum et al. (2019), in their study, emphasised that storytelling is useful in contemporary marketing based on the application of professionals and practitioners in giving credible narratives about products and services. According to Lamb et al. (2019), storytelling aims to make receivers of communication experience a cognitive feeling to the extent that it births inspiration to take decisive action.

Ultimately, the rise in usage and application of storytelling is to achieve promotional objectives that cover wider areas, like an increase in brand awareness based on the potential to relay brand stories like founders' experiences or brand or business success stories with authenticity, consciousness and humour. Equally, storytelling can easily achieve a persuasive objective in that the audience can be seamlessly convinced about an idea, experience or concept through rational arguments. In another vein, storytelling can tell and convey complex concepts and information through the telling of engaging tales or narratives.

When compared to traditional tools like advertising and modern tools like email and social media, storytelling promotes not only explicit information but also equally implicit feelings and experiences, and it provides a high likelihood that information will be learned and passed on by establishing it in a narrative framework.

Nigerian Experience

Growing up in the 1970s as a youngster was far different from the children that were born in the late 1980s and 1990s in all measures of socialisation, funfairs, merry-making and, most importantly, exposure to marketing advertisements for many products that were meant for children. For instance, only very few households could boast of a television set and radio, which made exposure to certain commercials impossible; thus, many children didn't know what they needed or wanted but were always at the mercy of their parents. Parents made recommendations and gave options to choices of products when they wanted to be fair, but in many cases, they imposed 'the affordable' on the children. By and large, many children had no contribution to what they consumed, but only what their parents brought home or recommended. This parental behaviour was not limited to children from low-income families; middle-class and upper-class parents were equally entwined in the cultures. The family decision making in the 1970s was parent-dominated which emanated in slogans like 'Mum say,' 'Dad bought this' or 'Uncle sent it,' hence children played lesser roles. So, it wasn't uncommon for children to be non-participatory in their buying decisions and choices. The foremost factor that fuelled this prevalence was the non-exposure of children to commercials or advertisements, unlike what the market began to experience in the mid-1980s. Truly, the 1970s was the era of 'Do not Touch,' a warning commonly issued by parents when it came to the operation of all electronic sets like the television and radio at home where a family was fortunate to have one.

When it comes to commercial advertisements and electronic sets at home, the 1970s had peculiar characteristics that seriously affected children's exposure to and assimilation of commercials. For instance, the first sets of televisions in the

1960s and 1970s were on pedestals that were about four to six feet high, which meant children would have to wait till an elderly person was around to switch them on. Secondly, it wasn't a 24-hour operation like we have today. Television stations opened by 4 p.m. and closed by 11.30 p.m. except on weekends and other days of public holidays television stations opened early by 8 a.m. and closed by 11.30 p.m. It was expected that children should be in bed by 8 p.m., so the exposure was limited. Also, only a few homes could boast of television sets. Many children had to walk down the streets to find a place to watch their favourite programmes. All these were peculiar to those who lived in cities and major towns, while those in the villages and hinterlands had no access to such media opportunities until they visited families in the cities and major towns. Equally, children's restrictions on the radio set came in different dimensions depending on the household's style; for instance, many parents caged the radio in a metal case and hung it on the wall where no youngster could reach it. Even the radiogram with a turntable radio always came with a lock, and the key was always kept away from the reach of the children. So, only parents had access to operate and control electronic sets, and in many cases, only the Daddies (the No-nonsense Dads).

According to Ade, a marketing executive in the Fast Moving Consumer Goods (FMCG) sector who was born in 1972 and is in his 50s now,

> I remembered many youngsters who had access to televisions came to school to relay the stories of movies and comedies watched to friends, and this further extended to commercial advertisements that were storytelling in nature e.g., Blue Band Margarine; Fa Soap; Bazooka Chewing Gum; Coke advertisements, etc.

Likewise, the radio commercials came with songs, comedies, rhymes or messages that many children who had access to sets memorised to relay to friends and teach colleagues who had no access to radio at home. Yet, organisations are still engaged in storytelling as a communication tool for brands, despite limited coverage. The effect of this was that a larger number of consumers looked up to the elites, the educated and the middle class, who had access to electronic sets, to make choices among brands for their consumption. This also affected children, whereby the 'none-exposed to commercials' looked up to the demand patterns of the 'exposed to commercials' to shape their buying behaviours.

The Case of Coke

Coke advertisements on television in the 1970s were largely foreign, yet storytelling. Unlike other commercial advertisement that were a combination of usage instructions and benefits, Coke was always about fun-making, partying, dancing and other interesting activities that easily caught the attention of children. Thus, it was easier for children who watched the advertisement on television to easily relay them to friends, which made children always look forward to attending a party where Coke would be shared to recreate the fun among themselves. This further whets the appetite of children for Coke, even when there were other brands to choose from. In many instances, children preferred a situation where two or three would share a bottle of 35 cl Coke with a bigger cupful of Tree Tops drink brand or other carbonated drinks with larger quantities just because they wanted to fit into the storyline in the storytelling commercials. The popular theme of the 1970s, 'I'd like to Buy the World a Coke' was a hit that equally had an impact on the Nigerian market. Other commercials of the 1970s were 'It is the Real Thing' and 'Refreshment,' which were inundated with dancing, hugging, sharing and friendship. This increased children's satisfaction with Coke not just from the taste but also from the fun of recreating the scenes in the commercials, like the style of dancing, acrobats and partying in family events among children, and it became more interesting and important when you were the one that got the bottle and not the cup.

Coke in the 1980s and 1990s

The economic boom of the 1980s opened the door for many Nigerian homes and households to acquire electronic gadgets, especially television sets and radios, as a sign of the improved standard of living. Socialisation and other forms of social acquaintance have improved astronomically in society. Children were not left out in the new economic prosperity, with nearly every household getting a TV set or radio, or at least a television and a radio in a large family or compound of many families. So, it was an era when children used to be glued to television sets to watch all programmes and enjoy many commercial advertisements.

The electronic media space witnessed many Coke commercials that embraced the typical storytelling style of the organisation. Aside from the popular themes in the period like 'Coke is it,' 'Have a Coke and a Smile,' 'Always Coca-Cola' and 'Refreshingly Different,' there were two landmark commercials that were on the lips of youngsters and children all through the 1980s and early 1990s.

One of the storytelling commercials of the 1980s that ran until earlier parts of the 1990s was the Coke Christmas commercial that dominated the screens, and it was tagged by many Nigerian families as the Coca-Cola version of Christmas Carol. The commercial came in two forms: The first one was the story of Santa with a long train in the Coca-Cola emblem and logo sharing the gifts of Coke bottles with people and equally reminding consumers of the importance of Coke during Christmas. Thereafter, a boy was with the mom for Christmas shopping, and he reminded her of the pack of Coke for Christmas. Impliedly, an average Nigerian youngster was made to believe that a Coke bottle is complementary to the Christmas menu. Consequently, it became a necessary request or to-do item for children who either followed their parents on Christmas shopping sprees or had the opportunity of being part of family decisions on the Christmas shopping list. Kemi, who is presently in her early 40s and a pharmaceutical marketing executive, remarked that her Christmas picture of 1986 was in a Santa costume and a bottle of Coke to fit into the depiction of Coca-Cola's Christmas image.

Another Christmas commercial that many people who grew up in the 1980s and early 1990s found memorable was Coca-Cola's Tomorrow People, which was the assemblage of children of different age groups from diverse national and racial backgrounds to form the choir.

> *I am the future of the world;*
> *I'm the hope of my nation,*
> *I'm tomorrow's people,*
> *. . .*

This commercial was commonly broadcast during the Christmas season, from the late 1980s to the early 1990s. Every child and teen looked forward to it; even those who had crossed the age of adulthood still relished the song and never planned to miss it. It was tagged Coca-Cola's version of Christmas Carol among many children in the country.

Another musical storytelling of Coca-Cola in the 1990s was the song:

> *Wherever there is a pool, there's a flirt.*
> *Whenever there's a school, there is homework,*
> *Whenever there's a beat, there is a drum,*
> *Whenever there's fun, there is Coca-Cola,. . .*
> *. . . . Whenever there's fun, there is Coca-Cola*

The song in Nigerian colloquial became an 'anthem' among children everywhere. It was not uncommon to stigmatise a youngster who could not sing the Coca-Cola theme as an unsocial being at schools, playgrounds or even at home among siblings or in a neighbourhood. It was an identity to be accepted among friends and associates.

Coke in the 2000s

The Coke commercial of a Brazilian boy in a typical Brazilian football team jersey who was playing football across the streets of Sao Paulo in Brazil, and from there he traversed to other parts of the world like Asia, the Middle East, Africa and Europe, and was being hailed by other youngsters till he got to the final destination with the ball to receive a bottle of Coke. The commercial was made in 2014, which was the year Brazil hosted the World Cup tournament. This commercial resonated with many Nigerian youngsters and football escapades, especially after the Nigerian U-17 team won the maiden Coca-Cola-sponsored U-17 World Cup and, subsequently, the U-21 World Cup, coupled with brilliant performances in other international competitions. The storyline behind the commercials reinvigorated a winning spirit in football competition among the youngsters; equally, it placed Coke in a special place in their preferences among carbonated drinks, and, importantly, the urge to recreate the Brazilian boy's prodigy in the commercial was more special and desirable among children in the game of football.

Another dimension in storytelling advertisements was the recent 'Share a Coke' theme, whereby consumers, mostly children and teens, were to look for their names on the Coke bottles. The commercial, either inadvertently or deliberately, created a sense of ownership and identity among the children in that they sought or charged vendors to get them a bottle of Coke with their names. The Share a

Coke commercial was received with tumultuous joy and acceptance among children, and this was evident at parties and events where children gathered. In many instances, children posed for photographs with the Coke bottles that bore their names as mementoes.

Coca-Cola Advertisement Budgets

One marketing variable and strategy that the management of Coca-Cola has relentlessly pursued is marketing communication, which to a certain extent is storytelling in operation and manifests in forms of entertainment, fun-creating, memorable, reminding, convincing and informative. Coca-Cola's global operation is divided into different markets, whereby each market is made up of the countries within the continent or other suitable modes for a homogenous market. Largely, this helps in operationalising marketing strategies, especially marketing communication. It isn't uncommon for advertisements and other commercials to recognise the peculiarities of each market/segment in terms of culture, languages, values, beliefs etc. For instance, nearly all the commercials are similar in theme, style, message and focus across the world, but the broadcast maintains the common language, values and culture of each market. In the same vein, the African market isn't left behind in these strategic operations; hence, advertisements and other commercials are broadcast in English, French or Portuguese, and the participants are black Africans in African costumes and environments, yet the same global broadcasts.

According to Statstic.com, Coca-Cola's global budgets for advertising are in billions of dollars to ensure the brand name of the organisation and its product line remain the consumers' favourites and top on the 'to-do list' (The Cable, 2017; Statista, 2024). See Figures 6.1a and 6.1b:

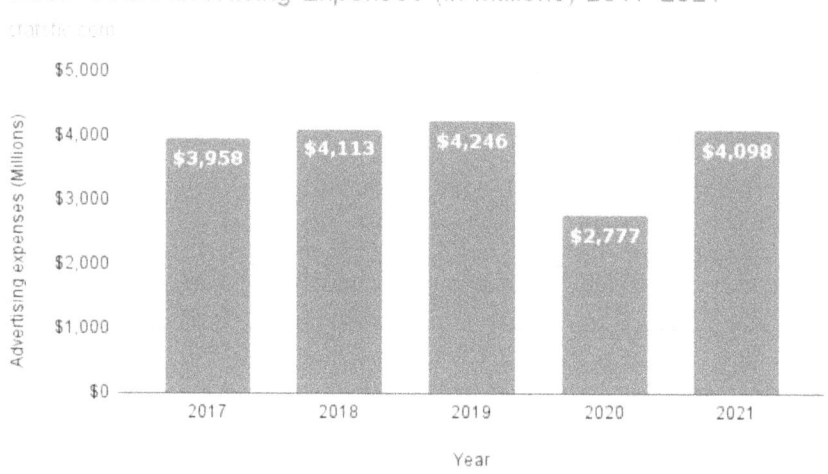

Figure 6.1 Coca-Cola advertising expenses (millions) 2017–2021.

Source: https://statstic.com/coca-cola-advertising-costs/

Storytelling: The Ethical Limits

The consideration of the connection between marketing communications and ethical issues is very germane to the conception and implementation of communication or promotional strategies in all organisations. In other words, it is strategically important for every organisation to know the point where the pursuit of a conviction, reminding and persuasion elements end to avoid litigation and penalties from both regulators and consumers alike. More importantly, the issue of ethical consideration needs to be seriously upheld when children constitute the largest percentage of consumers, especially when considering their innocence and tendency for impulsive purchases.

The critical areas of ethical issues that storytelling, if not well managed, may contravene are deception and hard selling (Jobber & Lancaster, 2011). The tendency is that narratives may be doctored to suit the sponsors' promotional objectives, hence deception. Also, the question remains: Is there a tendency for storytelling to lead to hard selling through high pressure and tactical execution in advertisement with high frequency and exposure?

Tuckwell (2005) and Shimp (2003) stressed the incidences of gender stereotyping, manipulative advertising and misleading advertising; hence, it is high time that advertising regulators and other market observers begin addressing the imminence of stereotyping in the execution of storytelling. For instance, a group of women's rights activists had to criticise the commercials of Nestle's Maggi Seasoning (which is mostly storytelling in nature) in the Nigerian market because, right from the inception, it focuses on women as the gender to cook. The critique is: 'Women's place is in the kitchen,' and the backlash is that young girls might underplay career pursuits in life, while young men may continue to see women as cooks alongside the housewives' responsibilities. Equally, the question of storytelling becoming manipulative and misleading, especially when children are mainly the audience or are involved in buying decisions, is imminent.

Will contemporary marketing communication experts, regulators and observers alike guarantee that the execution of storytelling as a marketing communication tool does not cross the borderline of ethical practice? This is a million-dollar question.

Questions

i. Assess any Alpha Generation product and the storyline communication associated with it in the light of ethical communication.
ii. Should Coca-Cola and other carbonated drink manufacturers maintain the present tempo of storytelling in marketing communication in light of

   a. Market share pursuit
   b. Ethical consideration
   c. Competitiveness in the market?

References

Jobber, D. & Lancaster, G. (2011). *Selling and Sales Management* (8th ed.). New York, United States of America: Pearson Publisher.

Lamb, C. W., Hair, J. F. & McDaniel, C. (2019). *Marketing* (15th ed.). Mason, United States of America: South-Western Cengage Learning.

Shimp, T. A. (2003). *Advertising, Promotion, & Supplementary Aspects of Integrated Marketing Communications* (6th ed.). Mason, OH, United States of America: Thomson, South-Western.

Tabassum, S., Khwaja, M. G. & Zaman, U. (2019). Can narrative advertisement and e-WOM influence generation-Z purchase intention? *Information (Switzerland)*, 11(12), pp. 1–16.

Tuckwell, K. J. (2005). *Integrated Marketing Communications: Strategic Planning Perspectives*. Toronto, Canada: Pearson-Prentice Hall.

Part 3

International Marketing

7   International Market Shaping

The Case Study of Indoor Hygiene
Solutions in Saudi Arabia

*Ibrahim A. A. AlZahrani, Saheed A. Gbadegeshin,
Zainurin B. Dahari and Rachid Moustaquim*

Introduction

In 2017, different organisations formed a consortium for a European Union Commission project named 'Indoor hygiene SME's Exports to the Middle East Construction Markets' (IHMEC). The commission funded the consortium through the Interreg Central Baltic program and the European Regional Development Fund. The consortium consisted of a lead partner, scientific partners and private companies from Finland, Sweden and Estonia. The lead partner is a university, as are the scientific partners. The private companies represent a variety of industries, which include construction materials, architecture, building technology and services, interior design and furniture. They were working on a project that offered innovative health solutions for public areas. Each private company has its own finished solution that it could just modify to suit its customers' needs and preferences. Thus, the project concept aimed to support these companies with a pool of indoor hygiene solutions from which customers could select to satisfy their needs. The solutions are related to all indoor elements, which consist of air, water and surfaces.

Background of the Case Study

The IHMEC project was a continuation of three previous projects: HYGTEC 1 and 2 and HygLi. The first project, HYGTEC 1, was research-based and focused on developing novel solutions from hygiene research. The project lasted for two years. It continued with the second project, HYGTEC 2, which focused on business concept development for the identified solutions. The positive result of the second project led to the third project, HygLi, which focused on the commercialisation of the novel solutions. In the third project, indoor hygiene solutions were confirmed to reduce the threat of pandemics and antibiotic-resistant microbes in indoor spaces. These projects were funded by the Finnish government agent for innovation, presently known as Business Finland and formerly known as 'Tekes.' The positive results of these projects energised the IHMEC, as its name suggested; the project aimed to develop novel and tailored indoor hygiene solutions and export them to the Middle East markets. The third project also tested novel solutions in the local (Nordic) market. To achieve its aim, the lead partner of IHMEC noticed how the

DOI: 10.4324/9781003441274-10

solutions could be combined as a pool and made available to the target customers to be selected from. This pool was termed an indoor hygiene solution package by the project consortium. This brief background shows how Finland has been working on indoor hygiene research. This effort made Finland the first country in the world to provide a guideline on planning, building and maintaining indoor hygiene (to the best of the knowledge of IHMEC project partners).

Indoor Hygiene Solutions

It is good to ask this question: ***What is an indoor hygiene?*** Let us start by defining 'indoor.' Indoor can refer to any space inside a building where people spend time, for example rooms (bedroom, living room, kitchen, toilet and bathroom), a lobby of a public building, a waiting area for services (like in restaurants, banks and train stations), a lecture room or auditorium in a university and an operating room of a hospital. Also, an indoor space refers to indoor air, surfaces and water (if there is a water outlet in the space). Furthermore, 'Hygiene' refers to anything that is clean, sanitary and conforms to healthcare requirements. Meanwhile, hygiene is no longer limited exclusively to healthcare and hospital-related contexts. For example, 'hand hygiene' is now commonly recognised. Proper hygiene is fundamental in every place such as schools, post offices, bus stations and supermarkets. Therefore, indoor hygiene means all activities that ensure the cleanliness of any indoor space. The activities include raising awareness, influencing knowledge, providing instructions, and developing and using hygiene solutions to prevent infections (IHMEC, 2023).

From the above-stated definitions, it can be agreed that indoor hygiene is paramount to every space these days with the recent coronavirus that trapped people to stay indoors for a long period of time. According to some studies, such as Pancani et al. (2021) and Klepeis et al. (2001), the majority of countries in the world locked down their people at home. These studies confirmed that more than 80% of people spent their time at home. These studies expressed that it was during the lockdown that many people realised the importance of indoor and personal hygiene. This is the reason why many scholars and medical practitioners are advising people to consider indoor hygiene, even from building design through the buildings' construction and maintenance, in order to keep the indoor environment healthy.

Also, the World Health Organization (2020) explained that hygiene is essential, specifically to deal with an increase in antibiotic resistance. This organisation expatiates that antibiotic resistance can affect anyone. It also expatiates that there is an increase in the number of infections, which consist of pneumonia, tuberculosis, gonorrhoea and salmonellosis. The organisation warns that the increase in antibiotic resistance will lead to longer hospital stays, higher medical costs and higher mortality. It advises that only proper hygiene can reduce and prevent these infections.

Finnish Indoor Hygiene Solutions to Kingdom of Saudi Arabia

In 2018, the consortium decided to export the indoor hygiene solution package to the Saudi Arabian construction market, using indoor hygiene as a competitive edge. An internationalisation expert, who focuses on the Saudi Arabia market, was hired. The expert joined the project in April 2018 and started working in May 2018. Before joining the project, the expert was briefed about the project and its goal, specifically shaping the Saudi Arabian market for its consortium's innovative solutions. As an expert, he first examined the project activities, conducted research and examined how indoor hygiene solutions would be applied in the Saudi Arabian market. He found that the solutions were highly suitable for the targeted market.

Meanwhile, *why Saudi Arabia but not other Middle East countries*? Firstly, Saudi Arabia is regarded as the largest economy in the region. It is also the only member of the G20 umbrella in the region. The economy of Saudi Arabia is primarily sustained by oil production and non-oil tourism, which includes the Hajj and Umrah. As a central religious point, Saudi Arabia witnesses a large volume of visitors on religious pilgrimages, seeking to experience the sacred mosques in Mecca and Madinah. Such guest traffic provides the economy with significant additional revenue. Hence, the use of innovative health solutions in public areas is fundamental because the country hosts millions of visitors annually during the religious tourism seasons and witnesses global mass gatherings (AlFattani et al., 2021). Although the country has the best knowledge of health control for mass gatherings, it is still vital to have comprehensive, innovative health solutions for public areas to prevent infection outbreaks and regulate health deterioration.

The findings of the internationalisation expert and the afore-mentioned reasons for Saudi Arabia led the consortium to initiate a discussion with different stakeholders in Finland. The discussions were successful and motivating. This was a turning point for actual international market-shaping. From this point, the consortium started to conduct preliminary activities, such as scanning the Saudi business environment, orienting Finnish market actors and discussing the intermediary market actors (e.g. the Saudi Arabian embassy in Finland and the Finland embassy in Saudi Arabia). After getting support from these intermediary market actors, the consortium focused on Saudi Arabian market actors. With the effort of an internationalisation expert, the Saudi Arabian market actors developed an interest in indoor hygiene solutions, and business relationships started between the consortium members, specifically the Finnish companies, and the Saudi Arabian market actors. This is how market-shaping started.

International Market Shaping

Thus, *what is market-shaping?* There are several definitions of market-shaping. The academic scholars described it from various perspectives. For this case study, market-shaping can be defined as a process that entails several activities conducted by market actors to initiate and manage various forms of change in their market. Again, *who are the market actors?* They are referred to as market stakeholders. They consist of individual persons, such as experts in different fields or industrial sectors, or a group of individuals like professional bodies. They also consist of private organisations, both profit-making and non-profit-making. They are composed of government and non-government organisations. The key feature of market actors is that they have the capability to influence changes in their market system (Baker & Nenonen, 2020; Nenonen & Storbacka, 2018).

Now, ***what is international market-shaping?*** This term is not widely discussed in the existing scholarly articles and books. One of the possible reasons might be that international market-shaping is closely related to internationalisation and international marketing. Another reason might be that the scholars focus very much on local market-shaping. Nevertheless, in this case, international market-shaping is described as an effort to influence a foreign market, especially by entering, penetrating, creating and maintaining the international market. This entails the process of conducting business activities across borders that lead to an economic exchange.

Having explained the key terms of the case study, the consortium started their international market-shaping by conducting several activities, which include visiting Saudi Arabia, organising different workshops and meetings, and participating in conferences and workshops. The activities also include the hosting of Saudi Arabian stakeholders in Finland and showing references. References here refer to visits to places where the indoor hygiene solutions were used in Finland to show the functionality and added values of the solutions. This phase of international market-shaping is regarded as the initiation phase.

After a few months of market-shaping initiation, the shaping activities set in. They include the establishment of business relations, communications and business negotiations. These activities took several months. Fortunately, the third phase came in when there was an order from a Saudi Arabian distributor. The order was for five products from one of the Finnish companies to prove the concept and examine the interests of the Saudi stakeholders. Processing and delivering the order are regarded as the post-shaping phase. This phase was full of discussions and meetings to ensure a smooth business transaction.

Also, at the post-shaping phase, the consortium and the internationalisation experts reflected on their international market-shaping process. They discussed their lessons, which consisted of both things that went well and those that went wrong. One of their activities that were successful was visiting and having meetings with Saudi Arabian stakeholders. The consortium affirmed that the trip enabled them to have an understanding of their target market, become familiar with it and create social or business networks. Similarly, one of the issues that they faced was modification of the indoor solutions. The consortium noted that the weather conditions in Finland or most of Europe are different from those in the Middle East, specifically temperature. The consortium tried to manage how the solutions could be adjusted to the international market's preferences and standards.

Furthermore, the consortium documented that they learned a lesson about cultural dynamics when they were outlining the process and the challenges. The consortium noted that the cultural dynamics, which include institutional and individual cultural dynamics in Saudi Arabia, are essential to be understood for any foreign businesses that want to operate in the country. For instance, the consortium for the case project was used to the European business culture and had not previously visited Saudi Arabia. When they had to visit the Kingdom of Saudi Arabia, they were informed on how they introduced themselves, acted and things to avoid.

Specifically, they were informed to use their title when visiting Saudi Arabia. Similarly, they were informed about handshaking in Saudi Arabia. They were informed that 'when meeting and greeting in Saudi Arabia, it is usual for close male counterparts to shake hands and kiss each cheek. However, if the meeting is informal, a handshake between members of the same sex is fine.' All these issues sound simple, but they were considered important during reflection.

The above reflection made the consortium realise that international market-shaping heavily depends on innovative solutions because innovations have no borders. The consortium learned that when an organisation, either small or big, has an innovation that solves a specific problem, such an entity can shape an international market. Meanwhile, the consortium suggested that the initial innovation might need to be refined or improved to suit the international market (segments). If this situation happens, the shaping process does not need to start from the initiation phase; it needs to start from the shaping phase. The consortium concluded that international market-shaping is a continuous process, like a chain, until a new technology disrupts the chain.

Can Saudi Arabian Market Dynamics Speak for the Larger Middle East Market?

As it was mentioned earlier, Saudi Arabia is the largest economy in the Middle East. Apart from being an important economy, the country is a key member of the Cooperation Council for the Arab States of the Gulf (GCC, 2023), which shares common political and economic values. The GCC consists of Bahrain, Kuwait, Oman, Qatar, Saudi Arabia and the United Arab Emirates. The GCC is similar to the European Union in Europe and the Economic Community of West African States in Africa. Also, this economic union shows that member countries share common weather conditions, religions and policies. Hence, being an important member of the GCC shows that the Saudi Arabian market speaks for the GCC market. It means that a product or service that is accepted in Saudi Arabia could be easily sold in the GCC area without too many bureaucratic procedures, such as language translation, religion consideration and transportation.

Furthermore, Saudi Arabia is a member of the Arab League, which is another intergovernmental organisation. According to Council on Foreign Relations (2023), Arab League comprises of Arab-speaking countries across two continents, Africa and Asia: Algeria, Bahrain, Comoros, Djibouti, Egypt, Iraq, Jordan, Kuwait, Lebanon, Libya, Mauritania, Morocco, Oman, Palestine, Qatar, Saudi Arabia, Somalia, Sudan, Syria, Tunisia, the United Arab Emirates and Yemen. The member countries do regard Saudi Arabia as their centre and economic power. Thus, products or services accepted in Saudi Arabia might easily be marketed in the countries of the Arab League.

In addition, several studies establish that there is a little difference between the consumer behaviour of GCC and Arab League countries due to their commonality, specifically Islam. In view of this, the Saudi Arabian market seems to speak for the Middle East and its neighbouring regions, such as North Africa and Asia. This was one of the reasons that the IHMEC consortium decided to shape the Saudi Arabian market.

Conclusion

So far, this case study has shown how innovative solutions could be used to shape an international market that you might not be familiar with. The case study also enlightened you about indoor hygiene and its importance for our lives. It also introduced you to market-shaping and processes. Thus, the case study is educational. Hence, as a business student, entrepreneur, businessperson and future entrepreneur, you can ponder the following questions:

a) *Do you think that international market-shaping would be a better option for a new business or growing-up company?*
b) *What are the important issues to consider while thinking of shaping an international market?*
c) *What could be the challenges for shaping an international market?*

Providing answers to the aforementioned questions enables you to have an overview of international market-shaping, which is becoming an important phenomenon in today's business environment. As we all know, the business environment is no longer stable and predictable. The outbreak of the COVID-19 that affected the global economy coupled with the unimaginable Russia-Ukraine war are examples of unexpected circumstances that make the business environment unstable. Therefore, using the case study to process and understand the international market-shaping would help to prepare your minds for the future when exploring business opportunities that emerge from market instability or disruption.

References

AlFattani, A., AlMeharish, A., Nasim, M., AlQahtani, K. & AlMudraa, S. (2021). Ten public health strategies to control the COVID-19 pandemic: The Saudi experience. *IJID Regions*, 1, pp. 12–19.

Baker, J. J. & Nenonen, S. (2020). Collaborating to shape markets: Emergent collective market work. *Industrial Marketing Management*, 85, pp. 240–253.

The Cooperation Council for the Arab States of the Gulf (GCC, 2023). Available at: https://www.gcc-sg.org/en-us/Pages/default.aspx (Accessed on 1 June 2023).

Council on Foreign Relations. (2023). *The Arab League*. Available at: https://www.cfr.org/backgrounder/arab-league (Accessed on 1 March 2023).

IHMEC. (2023). *Indoor Hygiene Solutions*. Available at: https://ihmec.fi/about/ (Accessed on 1 March 2023).

Klepeis, N. E., Nelson, W. C., Ott, W. R., Robinson, J. P., Tsang, A. M., Switzer, P., . . . & Engelmann, W. H. (2001). The National Human Activity Pattern Survey (NHAPS): A resource for assessing exposure to environmental pollutants. *Journal of Exposure Science & Environmental Epidemiology*, 11(3), pp. 231–252.

Nenonen, S. & Storbacka, K. (2018). *Smash: Using Market Shaping to Design New Strategies for Innovation, Value Creation, and Growth*. Emerald Group Publishing, London.

Pancani, L., Marinucci, M., Aureli, N. & Riva, P. (2021). Forced social isolation and mental health: A study on 1,006 Italians under COVID-19 lockdown. *Frontiers in Psychology*, 12, p. 1540.

World Health Organization (WHO). (2020). *Antibiotic Resistance*. Available at: https://www.who.int/en/news-room/fact-sheets/detail/antibiotic-resistance (Accessed on 1 March 2023).

8 Going Global – A Qualitative Analysis of Nigerian Cuisine Beyond the 'Jollof Rice' Rivalry

Nnamdi O. Madichie

Introduction

This case is based on my treatise on Nigerian Restaurants Worldwide, which captures the core of the debate on two key themes (marketing communications and international/global marketing), especially as it chronicles the internationalisation of the restaurant sub-sector of the food industry beyond the shores of Nigeria. From a broad review of the literature and content analysis of media reports, the narrative is weaved together and provides some teaching and research implications for studying ethnic food marketing. Three countries in particular are touched upon: the UK (the United Kingdom), the UAE (United Arab Emirates) and Rwanda. In terms of managerial and theoretical implications, 'Nigerian restaurateurs need to up their game and provide the appropriate ambience, quality of service and innovativeness,' a theme that resonates with my inaugural research, 'Nigerian restaurants in London: bridging the experiential perception/expectation gap' published in 2007. At the theoretical level, academics are encouraged to prompt students to undertake research projects on how to internationalise/globalise ethnic cuisine (e.g. Nigerian restaurants competitiveness, especially in markets or economies outside Nigeria).

Three countries in particular are touched upon: the UK (the United Kingdom), the UAE (United Arab Emirates) and Rwanda. The chapter is based on a combination of documentary evidence and the lived experiences of the author spanning over a decade, with a view to calling out potential startups and/or investors in the hospitality sector. It also includes some narrative, discourse and archival research elements alongside storytelling (Farrant, 2014; Iseke, 2013; Lewis, 2011; Bailey & Tilley, 2002).

Nigerian Restaurants in London: Bridging the Experiential Perception/Expectation Gap

Nigerians in the diaspora know the exact needs of their siblings at home visiting these new climes. But the question is how they have responded to this clientele. I have lived in Dubai, London and Scotland and visited Berlin, Houston, Atlanta, Florida, Tanzania and South Africa in the past decade or so. In these journeys and sojourns, I have been rather unimpressed by the ambience of Nigerian restaurants

DOI: 10.4324/9781003441274-11

in these locations (when compared with their counterparts). There is a Nigerian saying that the way to a man's heart is through food. The same can be said about the best therapy for homesickness. Is food the only attraction? How about the atmosphere? Attitude of the waiters/waitresses? Customer service?

This chapter was pitched as a wake-up call with managerial and theoretical implications. At the managerial level, Nigerian restaurateurs need to up their game and provide the appropriate ambiance, quality of service and innovativeness. At the theoretical level, academics should encourage students to undertake research projects on how to make Nigerian restaurants competitive, especially in climes outside Nigeria.

Silent Voices in Rwanda: The Case of Danfo by the Grid. An Uphill Task in the Land of a Thousand Hills

Another article in the series of Nigerian Restaurants Worldwide has been a long time coming. In my last two explorations, Rwanda was the last thing on my mind (Madichie, 2019a, 2019b). Lately, however, something did happen in the reputable and upmarket Kigali Business Centre (now renamed Kigali Alliance Business Centre or KABC). While 'Danfo by The Grid' may well be a 'new entrant' following in the footsteps of Jollof Kigali, there are some interesting differences. Unlike the former, the latter (Jollof Kigali) has a bit more space and an enviable selection of Nigerian beverages, both alcoholic and non-alcoholic. Looking at both restaurants, however, there are some pros and cons. While location and atmosphere have been deemed central to the competitiveness of businesses, especially those providing services such as food marketing and others, they may not be the only criteria for customers and/or clientele. For *Danfo by the Grid*, the location is sublime; KABC is a prime location next to the famed Kigali Heights retail complex and the revered events venue, Kigali Convention Centre, but it is arguably less vibrant than the pioneer, Jollof Kigali, which offers so much more (Madichie, 2023).

Building on the first of the series in this treatise, Madichie (2019a) writes in the article, 'Nigerians in the diaspora know the exact needs of their brothers and sisters at home visiting these new climes. But the question is how have they responded to these clientele?' Against the backdrop of the author's diaspora sojourn – having lived in Dubai, London, Scotland and visited Berlin, Houston, Atlanta, Florida, Tanzania and South Africa in the past decade or just over – the ambience of Nigerian restaurants in these locations, when compared with their counterparts, has been below par.

Desert Dessert: Nothing Posh in the UAE

A follow-on article (see Madichie, 2019b) considered the exploits of Nigerian restaurants in the Middle East, notably Dubai, the acclaimed preferred travel destination for Nigerians. Although there is never any verifiable evidence of population numbers for this group, even though the country's population relies on estimates of anything between 170 million and 200 million, various sources tend to suggest that there are at least about 5,000 Nigerians resident in the United Arab Emirates (UAE), with most of them based in Dubai. This seems to exclude the number of Nigerians studying in the country.

It is a wonder just how Nigerian restaurants are faring in Dubai and its environs (e.g. Abu Dhabi, Sharjah and even Ajman). Not very well, I dare say. These emirates (or city states with the UAE) seem to be the forte of South Asians (notably India, Pakistan and Bangladesh).

As Madichie (2019b) further points out, going further down the pecking order and even from those areas geographically defined (the socio-political definition seems to be somewhat different as many of these nationals tend to see themselves as Arab) as African, for example Comoros, Egypt, Morocco, Sudan and Tunisia. As for Nigerian restaurants, they seem to be operating at the lowest rungs of ambience. Sometimes one would wonder whether to tuck in at all after a site visit to places like the Gold Souk, Deira, Al Nahda and Al Sabkha (a small community between Al Rigga, Naif, Al Dhagaya and Al Buteen) in the Deira region of eastern Dubai. Is it really surprising that no 'African' restaurant comes close in the top-10 listing? Not even the much-celebrated KIZA that claims to be Pan-African (with Swahili undertones) comes across as being authentically Nigerian, and that is where the confusion lies.

Located in the Mall of the Emirates and Dubai Mall in the UAE, Tribes Restaurant, for example is a fun, casual dining restaurant with a menu inspired by the amazing food and flavours of Africa, an extremely diverse continent with numerous tribes that not only speak different languages but also have very different foods that they prepare and serve to their family and friends with a lot of pride.

Still on the upmarket offerings, here is another one, Africana Home, which claims the following history: Africana Home Restaurant is the UAE's first African kitchen. The restaurant first opened its doors in 1993 to the delight of customers craving tasty African cuisine and has continued to provide a home-away-from-home feeling. Why is it that Nigerian restaurants continue to operate from one-bedroom apartments?

Discussions

This chapter pulls together a treatise by the author on how Nigerian restaurants worldwide have been faring beyond the shores of the country. On the basis of personal observations and the sojourn of the author across three locations – that is London, Dubai and Kigali – the chapter sheds light on the competitiveness of Nigerian cuisine. The chapter observes and reports that ethnic food is a force majeure for diasporic life. Having encountered numerous Nigerians visiting the United Kingdom and London in particular, who no sooner than they unpacked their travel gear, sought answers to the age-long question, 'Is there any Nigerian eatery nearby?' While this may have often occurred as a bit of a shock to the author, who imagined that only a few hours ago, these individuals would have treated themselves to some variant of Nigerian food, from the more renowned jollof rice to pounded yam and vegetable soup (edikang kong, okro, ogbono, ewedu or bitter leaf) and suya or fish or goat meat and pepper soup.

In the second part of the treatise, Madichie (2019b) interrogated the trend in the context of the Middle East, and notably the famed travel destination of Nigerians, that is Dubai, the acclaimed preferred travel destination for Nigerians (aka Naija). Although there is never any verifiable evidence of population numbers for this group, even though the country's population relies on estimates of anything between 170 million and 200 million, various sources tend to suggest that there are at least about 5,000 Nigerians resident in the United Arab Emirates (UAE), with most of them based in Dubai. This seems to exclude the number of Nigerians studying in the country (Madichie, 2019b).

Nigerians really love their food that much; as I pointed out in my last post, are they really being served? And yes, I ask this literally, if you are wondering. I posed a similar question many years ago in my 2007 paper on Nigerian restaurants in London, which I have only recently tried to reconceptualise in a post highlighting the challenges of African Caribbean restaurants in London.

Having lived in the UAE for nearly a decade and besides this personal first-hand experience, you may wish to read the message of the managing director, a notable player:

> Africana Home, whom I assume to be the founder below: When I first came to the UAE, I was unused to the taste and flavour of the food, although many tried to be as hospitable as they could but a lot was lacking, I just couldn't stand it, And so the Vision for Africana Home was birthed. From a one-bedroom apartment, cooking for friends, colleagues, and neighbours, to a small restaurant space with just three employees, to a thriving chain of restaurants, we truly have come from humble beginnings.

Regrettably, only a few seem to have transitioned from such 'humble beginnings,' as numerous other Nigerian 'restaurants' (deliberately in quotation marks) are still operating under the radar in the most squalid of conditions. What is more? Filipino restaurants have started making inroads in the country with the recent announcement by the Al Ahli Holding Group for a new chain of Filipino restaurants, Little Manila restaurant, in September at Al Muraqqabat Street, Deira, offering a variety of Filipino dishes, from Fruitas, Mochi Créme, Zagu to the popular dish Binalot, grilled meat and rice on banana leaves. According to Parvez Naqvi, the International Business Development Head for Al Ahli Holdings Group:

> The idea behind Little Manila was to give the third largest expat community in the GCC an exposure to experience the flavours of their home country while staying in the Middle East and to give them a chance to come together as a community to call a place their own.

Recently, Gbemi Giwa's new health-oriented African restaurant, Catfish, which operates out of the Kitchen Nation incubator space in the exclusive Business Bay area of Dubai, has been heart-warming. However, the question still remains, why are Nigerian restaurants in Dubai still very few and far between? One of the series on Nigerian Restaurants Worldwide has been a long time coming.

Against the backdrop of my diaspora sojourn – having lived in Dubai, London, Scotland and visited Berlin, Houston, Atlanta, Florida, Tanzania and South Africa in the past decade or just over – I have been rather unimpressed by the ambience of Nigerian restaurants in these locations (when compared with their counterparts).

Another eye-catcher is the creative naming convention of the cocktails, which highlights/celebrates everything Lagos, from 'Lagos Island' to 'Ikeja Margaritas.'

- LAGOS ISLAND (Rum, Vodka, Gin, Coke, Triple sec, Tequila, Lime juice).
- OJUELEGBA MOJITO (Mint Leaves, Brown sugar, Rum, Soda water, Wedges, Choice of fruit).
- ELEGUSHI DAIQUIRI (Strawberry puree, Strawberry syrup, Lime juice, Vodka).
- ALLEN AVENUE WHISKY SOUR (Wild turkey bourbon, Lemon Juice, Simple syrup and Egg White).
- OLOSHO WHISKY (Lemon juice, Jameson, Sprite, Lemon wedges).
- IKEJA MAGARITA (Tequila, Triple sec, Lime juice and Choice of fruit).

Last but surely not least, the jollof rice is awesome, irrespective of who won the debate over this popular Nigerian dish.

Taking the Conversation Further – A Message From the Conversation

The authorship – and therefore origins – of jollof rice (called ceebu jën in Senegal according to the Wolof spelling) is the subject of a spicy debate between West African nations. In particular, Senegalese, Nigerians and Ghanaians claim ownership. And each believes their recipe surpasses all others (Niang, 2023). At the end of 2021, UNESCO included the Senegalese version of jollof rice – *ceebu jën* – on the intangible heritage of humanity list. This certification was a recognition of the expertise of the Senegalese as an integral part of an intangible heritage. The labelling should also have a positive impact on the economy, particularly in tourism, agriculture, fishing and catering, or, as some would describe it, gastro-diplomacy (Niang, 2023).

But to make the most of all these advantages, Senegal must pay more attention to its fishery resources and, above all, settle the recurrent question of self-sufficiency in rice production for good in order to put an end to the scandalous perversion of feeding on what is not produced (Niang, 2023).

Senegal, whose reputation is based more on its cultural influence and diplomacy, has every interest in capitalising on this trend. Thus, in addition to rice with fish, it will have to promote its broader gastronomic heritage to make it an additional asset for the role it intends to play in the concert of nations. In this spirit, Senegal's Food Technology Institute would be given a new lease of life. This public establishment, created in 1963, was assigned the mission of research and development in food and nutrition.

Conclusion

This case is based on my treatise on Nigerian Restaurants Worldwide, which captures the core of the debate on two key themes (marketing communications and international/global marketing), especially as it chronicles the internationalisation of the restaurant sub-sector of the food industry beyond the shores of Nigeria. From a broad review of the literature and content analysis of media reports, the narrative is weaved together and provides some teaching and research implications for studying ethnic food marketing.

Three countries in particular are touched upon: the UK (the United Kingdom), the UAE (United Arab Emirates) and Rwanda. In terms of managerial and theoretical implications, 'Nigerian restaurateurs need to up their game and provide the appropriate ambience, quality of service and innovativeness' a theme that resonates with my inaugural research, 'Nigerian restaurants in London: bridging the experiential perception/expectation gap' published in 2007. At the theoretical level, academics are encouraged to prompt students to undertake research projects on how to internationalise/globalise ethnic cuisine (e.g. Nigerian restaurants competitiveness, especially in climes outside Nigeria).

There are managerial and theoretical implications. 'Nigerian restaurateurs need to up their game and provide the appropriate ambience, quality of service and innovativeness' is a theme that resonates with my inaugural research, 'Nigerian restaurants in London: bridging the experiential perception/expectation gap' published in 2007. At the theoretical level, academics should encourage students to undertake research projects on how to make Nigerian restaurants competitive, especially in climes outside Nigeria.

Figure 8.1 Another brand name of a Nigerian-owned restaurant that was derived from a popular means of transportation in Nigeria – Danfo.

Figure 8.2 A Nigerian-owned restaurant brand name that is derived from the name of a Nigerian major city of Lagos – Made in Lagos.

Figure 8.3 Typical Nigerian cuisine – jollof rice and pepper soup.

References

Bailey, P. H. & Tilley, S. (2002). Storytelling and the interpretation of meaning in qualitative research. *Journal of Advanced Nursing*, 38(6), pp. 574–583.

Farrant, F. (2014). Unconcealment: What happens when we tell stories. *Qualitative Inquiry*, 20(4), pp. 461–470.

Iseke, J. (2013). Indigenous storytelling as research. *International Review of Qualitative Research*, 6(4), pp. 559–577.

Lewis, P. J. (2011). Storytelling as research/research as storytelling. *Qualitative Inquiry*, 17(6), pp. 505–510.

Madichie, N. (2019a, October 13). Nigerian restaurants worldwide: A research agenda part 1. *Tekedia*. Available at: https://www.tekedia.com/nigerian-restaurants-worldwide-a-research-agenda-part-1/

Madichie, N. (2019b, November 10). Nigerian restaurants worldwide: A research agenda part 2. *Tekedia*. Available at: https://www.tekedia.com/nigerian-restaurants-worldwide-a-research-agenda-part-2/

Madichie, N. (2023, February 6). Nigerian restaurants worldwide: A research agenda part 3. *Tekedia*. Available at: https://www.tekedia.com/nigerian-restaurants-worldwide-a-research-agenda-part-3/

Niang, F. (2023). Who invented jollof rice? Senegal beats Ghana and Nigeria to the title Published: January 18. *The Conversation*, Available at: https://theconversation.com/who-invented-jollof-rice-senegal-beats-ghana-and-nigeria-to-the-title-197352

Part 4

Entrepreneurship Marketing

9 Entrepreneurial Marketing Strategies

The Case of Ghanaian Artisans in Suame Magazine

Atsu Nkukpornu, Etse Nkukpornu and Kwame Adom

Why Entrepreneurial Marketing

The concepts of marketing and entrepreneurship, hitherto, were treated in silos. In recent times, there has been a call for the integration of both concepts (Arshi et al., 2023). The ideas presented here follow this theme of putting entrepreneurship into marketing (Strokes, 2000). This has become necessary due to the intense competition that characterises businesses, particularly in the artisanal sector. In Ghana, there are two major artisanal hubs (Abossey Okai and Suame Magazine).

The Abossey Okai is a bustling neighbourhood in Accra, Ghana, known for its vibrant marketplaces and diverse artisans. The area is known for its automobile spare parts trade, making it a popular destination for those seeking automotive components and accessories. Abossey Okai skilled craftsmen manufacture local cars known as 'Abossey Okai Matwo.' Matwo, in the local language, means strongest. Therefore, the name of the local truck is translated to mean 'Abossey Okai strongest.' The area is referred to as the 'car parts hub' of Africa. The area attracts both locals and visitors seeking quality products at competitive prices.

The 'Suame Magazine' is a prominent establishment situated in the Ashanti Region of Ghana and is located precisely in Suame, Kumasi. Suame Magazine is known as the 'Detroit of West Africa' (Gatune, 2016). This artisanal hub is made up of skilled artisans and craftsmen who are specialised in producing machinery and transforming their small workshops into centres of ingenuity (Adeya, 2008). The ambiance of Suame Magazine is characterised by a cacophony of sounds, creating a captivating and industrious atmosphere. Suame Magazine is widely recognised as one of the most prominent informal automobile industrial clusters in the West African region. The skilled artisans in Suame Magazine also manufacture a local car called 'Boafour,' which means helper.

The artisans in both Abossey Okai and Suame Magazine exhibit expertise in diverse automotive trades, encompassing metalworking, welding, panel beating, auto electrical, upholstery and mechanics. The individuals have refined their skills through practical application and mentorship, cultivating a high level of proficiency in distinct domains of automotive maintenance and modification. To remain abreast of the ever-changing automotive technologies, individuals consistently enhance their skills and techniques, enabling them to effectively diagnose and rectify

DOI: 10.4324/9781003441274-13

contemporary vehicle systems and components; exhibit a profound reverence for traditional craftsmanship and practices and embrace innovation. The organisation places a significant emphasis on the preservation of heritage techniques and traditional knowledge, which are thoughtfully integrated with contemporary technologies to provide exceptional repairs and customisation services of superior quality. They possess entrepreneurial skills and actively oversee the operations of their workshops or businesses.

Though these artisanal hubs remain in the informal sector, their contributions to the socio-economic fortunes of the Ghanaian economy cannot be underestimated in terms of job creation and poverty alleviation. Notwithstanding the achievements, the market or business ecosystem where these artisans operate is characterised by intense competition, environmental uncertainties and resource constraints.

Captivatingly, these artisans exhibit exceptional craftsmanship and entrepreneurial qualities, recognising the importance of marketing in enhancing their enterprises. However, little has been documented regarding the EM strategies employed by the artisans. This case study seeks to shed light on the EM strategies employed by Ghanaian artisans to navigate their businesses and achieve success in a resource-constrained and fiercely competitive environment. This study has become necessary because existing studies on understanding EM have focused on businesses in the developed context, with a paucity of literature looking at businesses at the micro-level in developing economies.

The comprehension of the EM from an artisanal perspective from Ghana will significantly contribute to existing scholarship. First, it will enable researchers, educators and professionals to enhance the efficacy of marketing strategies for entrepreneurial endeavours. Second, the integrated perspective can inform the development of context-specific educational curricula and programmes that equip entrepreneurs with essential marketing knowledge and skills while capitalising on their unique entrepreneurial strengths.

The question that needs to be answered is: What EM strategies are employed by artisans in the entrepreneurial ecosystem in Ghana to gain competitive advantage in a highly turbulent business environment and resource-constrained environment? The authors seek to provide answers to the question by using artisans in 'Suame Magazine' located in Kumasi, Ghana.

The chapter is structured in the following manner: First, we analyse the definition of 'EM' and its significance in the context of the current discourse. The authors looked at how the data were collected from the artisans of Suame Magazine. The authors present EM strategies from a perspective that focuses on artisans, especially spare parts dealers, in a Ghanaian context and provide detailed explanations of their unique features. The study looked at the implications of EM for Ghanaian entrepreneurs and identified key areas for future research that could shape the future of the EM field.

What Is Entrepreneurial Marketing?

Academic literature suggests a disconnect between marketing and entrepreneurship, leading to efforts to merge the two fields through the development of EM or Small and Medium Scale Enterprises (SME) marketing (Lam & Harker, 2015, p. 341). EM is a new paradigm that integrates critical aspects of marketing and entrepreneurship into a comprehensive concept where marketing becomes a process used by firms to act entrepreneurially to find solutions to tough and unstable environmental situations (Arshi et al., 2023; Sadiku-Dushi et al., 2019). In other words, EM is a hybrid concept of entrepreneurship and marketing that defines business for future challenges (Dubey et al., 2020).

Scholars have made significant contributions regarding the definition of EM and its importance to young business success in dynamic and resource-constrained environments (Arshi et al., 2023; Fink et al., 2020; Hallbäck & Gabrielsson, 2013). EM is a proactive and innovative concept related to customer-perceived quality for business growth and excellence. According to Arshi et al. (2023), EM is conceptualised as a set of processes for creating, communicating and delivering value to customers and managing customer relationships in ways that benefit the organisation and its stakeholders. EM aims to create customer value and equity, build and renew competitive value, seek profitability and overcome challenges in uncertain economic times (Fink et al., 2020). EM is also considered a knowledge-based capability that can help International New Ventures achieve post-entry performance by adapting to market dynamism and reconfiguring their resources and capabilities. The concept of EM is considered powerful in describing smaller, younger and resource-constrained entrepreneurial firms (Hallbäck & Gabrielsson, 2013).

How Was the Data Collected?

The study presented a picture of the two major artisanal hubs in Ghana (i.e. Abossey Okai and Suame Magazine). However, this case study is focused on Suame Magazine. Suame Magazine is located at the foot and side of a hill, to the west of a cove, and east of the main route connecting Kumasi with Ghana's northern regions. The authors interviewed five (5) 'masters' who are leaders of the artisanal units (like spare parts dealers, auto mechanics, welders and metal workers, auto electricians and upholstery). Suame Magazine is an open-gated artisanal ecosystem. Therefore, an informal approach is required. One of the masters was contacted for the interview, and he instructed his apprentices to call other masters to join the interview. In Suame Magazine, the mode of entry is through apprenticeship. As a result, every master in Suame Magazine has gone through an apprenticeship and has a grasp of knowledge in the field to be the mouthpiece of the sector he or she represents. Due to the busy and noisy nature of the workplace, the interview was handwritten, with notes on key points. The interview lasted for 25 minutes. After the interview, what was written was narrated to the interviewees, and they confirmed it as a true reflection of their responses. The artisans were informed about the purpose of the interview, and they consented to participate. Akan (Ashanti Twi) was used as the local language for the interview since Suame Magazine was located in Ashanti Region. And the local language spoken in the region is 'Ashanti Twi.' This enables the artisans to express themselves very well in the local language. Therefore, what is captured in this chapter is the literal transliteration.

What Entrepreneurial Marketing Strategies Are Used by Artisans in Suame Magazine?

Effectual Approach to Resource Mobilisation

Resourcefulness and creativity are prominently exhibited by artisans in Suame Magazine as a result of their constrained access to specialised equipment and limited resources. They employ creative strategies to address obstacles and constraints, frequently engaging in the production or restoration of components within the immediate vicinity in cases where the original parts are not easily obtainable (Nkukpornu & Nkukpornu, 2024).

Most of the artisans recount that

> it is difficult to get original parts to service faulty vehicles so what we have been doing is that we look at the part and we fabricate some to replace the faulty one. Also, import duties for spare parts for vehicles are skyrocketing day by day, even Covid-19 worsened the importation of vehicle spare parts, therefore, we are innovative and use the available spare parts and we do 'alterations' to the faulty part or if necessary, we fabricate new one to replace the faulty one.

The artisans admitted that they operate in a resource-constrained environment, yet they are not perturbed; rather, they resort to the resources at their disposal to achieve results. The application of an effectual approach to resource mobilisation in a business environment characterised by uncertainties and resource constraints is anchored in the effectuation theory proposed by Sarasvathy (Sarasvathy, 2001). This implies that artisans in Suame Magazine employ effectuation as a resource mobilisation technique. Thus, they use resources at their disposal to address faulty vehicles if original parts are not easily available.

Collaborations, Partnerships and Networks

As stated in our earlier submission, artisans in Ghana are not immune from resource scarcity. Another EM approach employed by artisans is collaborations, partnerships and networks. The Suame Magazine is distinguished by an ecosystem of artisans that emphasises collaboration and networking, they actively exchange knowledge, tools and resources to effectively accomplish intricate repair undertakings or address distinctive customer requirements. This network serves as a platform for the improvement of skills and encourages a collaborative approach to problem-solving. The entry mode is through an apprenticeship, where individuals are assigned to their masters to learn on the job for a designated period, depending on the area in which they intend to acquire skills.

The artisans stated that:

> For us we operate on the principle that '*one person's hand cannot cover the face of God*' so if a customer brings a problem and I cannot solve it alone, I called on other artisans with knowledge and skills in that area to assist. Even

This implies that the EM strategy that is working for the artisans is relationship building and positive WOMM through paying attention to customers, effective communication and swift delivery. What is happening in Suame Magazine is consistent with prior studies in different sectors.

For instance, in a study conducted by Oly Ndubisi in 2004, the focus was on examining the utilisation of relationship marketing (RM) within cultural contexts characterised by low power distance, collectivism, femininity, high uncertainty avoidance and long-term orientation. The research demonstrates that certain fundamental aspects of a relationship, including trust, equity, empathy and commitment, hold significant value in these cultural contexts. These values have the potential to foster customer repeat purchases, retention and sustained loyalty by providing superior customer value (Oly Ndubisi, 2004). The study conducted by Narteh et al. (2013) investigates the influence of RM on customer loyalty within the luxury and first-class hotel sectors in Ghana. The research employed a survey instrument that was administered to a sample of 300 guests of high-end and premium hotels in Ghana. The results indicate that there is a notable and favourable impact of six RM practices, specifically competence, commitment, conflict handling, trust, communication and relational bonds, on customer loyalty within the hotel industry in Ghana (Narteh et al., 2013). African entrepreneurs can improve customer satisfaction, loyalty and business growth through RM strategies.

Offline Marketing Channels

Although digital channels are experiencing increased prominence, it is important to note that traditional offline marketing channels continue to hold relevance in the Ghanaian context as they enable entrepreneurs to effectively engage with local audiences and establish credibility and confidence among prospective clients. Offline marketing involves using conventional marketing channels and tangible platforms, such as print advertisements, television and radio commercials, billboards, event sponsorships, brochures, flyers and telemarketing. The artisans featured in Suame Magazine often use offline marketing channels such as physical signs, banners and displays to bring in clients. These may be displayed outside of an artisan's workplace or storefront, and they highlight the artisan's area of expertise as well as their contact information and any other distinctive selling factors. The right kind of signage may attract the attention of passing customers and pique their interest in the things being offered.

The artisans interviewed said:

[O]ur local people cannot read so what we do is that we only draw the kind of vehicles or the activities we undertake on a board and place it on our storefronts. Most importantly we write our contact numbers very bold on the board. Some potential customers call the numbers and enquire about our area of specialty before they bring their cars.

These local and traditional channels enable artisans to establish a connection with potential customers through tangible and sensory encounters, which can yield positive outcomes in an environment with limited internet accessibility or low education and digital adoption rates. This localisation strategy enhances brand associations, communication efficacy and cultural understanding, which are crucial in African markets characterised by diverse cultural contexts (Oniku, 2016).

What Are the Implications of Entrepreneurial Marketing Strategies on Artisans in Ghana?

The aforementioned entrepreneurial strategies have diverse implications for artisans in Ghana, particularly those engaged in business activities within Suame Magazine. Suame Magazine artisans demonstrate resourcefulness and creativity by utilising effectiveness to mobilise resources effectively. This approach enables artisans to sustain their craftsmanship despite challenges in acquiring original components or high import costs. They offer repair and fabrication services using local resources, sustaining business operations and meeting customer needs. Also, Suame Magazine's artisans utilise collaborations, partnerships and networks to tackle limited resources and improve their skills. They exchange knowledge, tools and resources. Collaboration and networking imply that artisans can utilise collective expertise, enhance their capabilities and offer comprehensive solutions to customers.

In addition, artisans in Suame Magazine engage in the practice of product localisation and adaptation, wherein they modify their products or services to cater to the specific preferences of the local market. This process involves considering cultural nuances and affordability levels. Organisations can enhance market penetration and consumer acceptance by modifying product features, packaging and pricing strategies. Artisans modify and customise communal taxis, known as 'tro tros,' to meet the specific needs of the local transportation industry. This practice ensures the safety and comfort of passengers, prioritising their well-being and convenience. Artisans in metal fabrication create customised items that reflect their clients' social status and cultural beliefs. Artisans who adapt their products to local preferences are better equipped to meet customer needs, increase market demand and preserve cultural heritage.

Furthermore, the utilisation of WOMM and relationship building is a prominent EM strategy employed by artisans in Ghana to cultivate favourable publicity and establish credibility within the market. Artisans foster robust relationships and stimulate positive word-of-mouth promotion for their businesses by actively engaging with customers, delivering prompt service and prioritising customer satisfaction. In light of the limitations imposed by resource constraints on paid advertising, WOMM emerges as a viable and economically efficient strategy. The implication is that fostering robust customer relationships and capitalising on favourable word-of-mouth can facilitate customer loyalty, recurrent transactions and overall business expansion.

Finally, offline marketing channels continue to hold significance in the Ghanaian context, despite the increasing prominence of digital channels. Artisans operating within Suame Magazine employ various physical marketing strategies, such as signs, banners and displays, to effectively capture the attention of potential customers who may have limited access to the internet or exhibit low rates of digital adoption. Artisans can effectively convey their specialised skills and attract potential customers by strategically employing visual cues and prominently displaying contact information on their storefronts. This approach facilitates effective communication and encourages interested individuals to initiate inquiries. The suggestion is that offline marketing channels provide artisans with the opportunity to establish local connections, cultivate trust and effectively reach audiences in an environment where internet accessibility is restricted.

Conclusion, Future Research Direction

This case study highlights the EM strategies employed by artisans in Suame Magazine, an artisanal hub in Ghana. The artisans in this resource-constrained and fiercely competitive environment utilise various EM strategies to gain a competitive advantage and navigate their businesses successfully. These strategies include an effectuation approach to resource mobilisation, collaborations, partnerships and networks; product localisation and adaptation; word-of-mouth and RM; and the use of offline marketing channels. The findings of this case study contribute to our understanding of EM in the context of artisanal businesses in developing economies. It highlights the importance of integrating entrepreneurship and marketing to achieve business success in resource-constrained and competitive environments. The strategies employed by artisans in Suame Magazine can serve as valuable lessons for other entrepreneurs and researchers in similar contexts.

Future research in the field of EM in developing economies should explore and expand upon these findings. Due to context heterogeneity, further studies could investigate the effectiveness of specific EM strategies in different sectors and regions, examine the role of cultural factors in shaping marketing practices and explore the impact of technological advancements on artisanal businesses. Additionally, the research could focus on developing practical frameworks and guidelines for entrepreneurs in resource-constrained environments to effectively apply EM strategies.

What Are the Questions or Lessons for Business Students?

Business students interested in EM strategies by artisans in Suame Magazine, a renowned industrial hub in Kumasi, Ghana, can explore the following questions and lessons:

a. What are the unique characteristics and challenges faced by artisans in Suame Magazine?
b. What are the key elements of a successful marketing strategy for artisans in Suame Magazine?
c. What are the strategies for building and maintaining customer relationships in the artisanal market?
d. How can artisans in Suame Magazine effectively communicate the value and craftsmanship of their products?

e. How can artisans in Suame Magazine utilise local networks and partnerships for marketing and distribution?
f. What are the opportunities and challenges of expanding the market beyond local or regional boundaries?
g. How can artisans in Suame Magazine adapt their EM strategies to changing consumer preferences and trends?

Providing answers to these questions and lessons can help business students explore the unique context of Suame Magazine's artisanal market and gain insights into the EM strategies employed by artisans in the area.

References

Acheampong, G., Narteh, B. & Rand, J. (2017). Network ties and survival: A study of small commercial poultry farms in Ghana. *The International Journal of Entrepreneurship and Innovation*, 18(1), pp. 14–24.

Adeya, C. N. (2008). The Suame manufacturing cluster in Ghana. *Knowledge, Technology, and Cluster-Based Growth: Africa* (pp. 15–24). Washington, DC: The World Bank.

Arshi, T. A., Pleshko, L. P., Begum, V. & Butt, A. S. (2023). Can entrepreneurial marketing compensate for late market entry? A moderated mediation analysis. *Heliyon*, 9(5).

Dubey, P., Bajpai, N., Guha, S. & Kulshreshtha, K. (2020). Entrepreneurial marketing: An analytical viewpoint on perceived quality and customer delight. *Journal of Research in Marketing and Entrepreneurship*, 22(1), pp. 1–19.

Fink, M., Koller, M., Gartner, J., Floh, A. & Harms, R. (2020). Effective entrepreneurial marketing on Facebook–A longitudinal study. *Journal of Business Research*, 113, pp. 149–157.

Gatune, J. (2016). Suame magazine: The evolving story of Africa's largest industrial cluster. In O. Adesida, G. Karuri-Sebina & J. Resende-Santos (Eds.), *In Innovation Africa: Emerging Hubs of Excellence* (pp. 397–425). Leeds, UK: Emerald Group Publishing Limited.

Hallbäck, J. & Gabrielsson, P. (2013). Entrepreneurial marketing strategies during the growth of international new ventures originating in small and open economies. *International Business Review*, 22(6), pp. 1008–1020.

Lam, W. & Harker, M. J. (2015). Marketing and entrepreneurship: An integrated view from the entrepreneur's perspective. *International Small Business Journal*, 33(3), pp. 321–348.

Narteh, B., Agbemabiese, G. C., Kodua, P. & Braimah, M. (2013). Relationship marketing and customer loyalty: Evidence from the Ghanaian luxury hotel industry. *Journal of Hospitality Marketing & Management*, 22(4), pp. 407–436.

Nkukpornu, A. & Nkukpornu, E. (2024). Entrepreneurship realities in the light of COVID-19 in Ghana. In *The Future of Entrepreneurship in Africa* (pp. 11–22). Ghana: Productivity Press.

Oly Ndubisi, N. (2004). Understanding the salience of cultural dimensions on relationship marketing, it's underpinnings and aftermaths. *Cross Cultural Management: An International Journal*, 11(3), pp. 70–89.

ONIKU, A. C. (2016). Labelling in local language and its effect on consumer purchase decision of pharmaceutical products in Lagos Metropolis. *Nigerian Journal of Management Studies*, 17(1), pp. 157–166.

Quaye, D. M., Nkukpornu, A. & Acheampong, G. (2018). Brokering: Africa's unique brand of entrepreneurship. *African Entrepreneurship: Challenges and Opportunities for Doing Business*, pp. 261–274.

Sadiku-Dushi, N., Dana, L. P. & Ramadani, V. (2019). Entrepreneurial marketing dimensions and SMEs performance. *Journal of Business Research*, 100, pp. 86–99.

Sarasvathy, S. D. (2001). Causation and effectuation: Toward a theoretical shift from economic inevitability to entrepreneurial contingency. *Academy of Management Review*, 26(2), pp. 243–263.

Van Tonder, E., Petzer, D. J., Van Vuuren, N. & De Beer, L. T. (2018). Perceived value, relationship quality and positive WOM intention in banking. *International Journal of Bank Marketing*, 36(7), pp. 1347–1366.

10 Skyville Company Ltd.

A Case of Emerging Product in an Emerging Market

Ayodele C. Oniku and Owolabi L. Kuye

Introduction

The distinct differences between business operations in developed and emerging markets can be simple and complicated across industries. However, it becomes more complex when the interplay of business dynamism and environmental changes becomes the benchmark, especially the vagaries, acceptance and evolution of technology. Twenty-first-century business practices and operations are largely dominated and interrupted by the intertwining of technological advancement that is changing modes of operations at different levels across industries and consumer acceptance in different markets. Importantly, while organisations might be concerned about what is adaptable to the local market or the extent to which standardisation will fit into the local market, consumers' choice and acceptance are premised on different factors like disposable income, social class and status, culture and societal receptiveness to new technology; hence, the need to arrive at balance through market and consumer behaviour analyses for business success.

The issue of renewable energy, and more importantly, the clarion call that the world needs to embrace renewable energies as better sources for power generation and energy use and to save the earth, is no longer a developed world's palaver but a global concern. And while the developed world is embracing all the sources of renewable energy like wind energy, geothermal energy, hydro energy and bioenergy, many sub-Saharan African markets are largely tapping into solar power. The issues of technology transfer, manpower availability and government policy may hinder the operation and adaptation of many of the sources of renewable energy in many African economies and in the developing world at large.

Specifically, the Nigerian market has embraced solar power as a veritable, reliable and affordable alternative to renewable energy. However, its acceptance is not wholly about a reduction in emissions and pollution in society but, more importantly, as an alternative to epileptic power supply in the country that is largely sourced from hydroelectric energy.

The history of power or energy generation in Nigeria dates back to 1886, during colonial days. However, as social, economic and industrial developments grow, the need for an increase in the megawatts generated by the agencies involved becomes

DOI: 10.4324/9781003441274-14

inevitable. To a large extent, this was achieved at the initial stage, but as the rural electrification and connecting of many cities to the national grid continue, the government fails to increase the capacity generated to meet the national demand, which invariably leads to the present calamitous and epileptic power supply in the country. Today's Nigeria is in a state where having private power generators among households and industries is a must and necessity. A whole dependence on power supply from the national grid is tantamount to planning to fail or business closure on the part of industries, and resignation to discomfort and social alienation on the part of households and individual consumers.

Hitherto, NEPA, and later PHCN, which was formed in 1972 as a product of the merger of the Electricity Corporation of Nigeria (1951) and the Niger Dams Authority (1962), became the government agency that enjoyed the monopoly of power generation, transmission and distribution for many decades. The poor management of the corporation (the usual plight of government business in many developing countries) plunged the country's over 200 million population to rely on decried and unbelievable 12.522 MW largely sourced from thermal and hydro energy.

The Electric Power Sector Reform that was signed in 2005 birthed a new marketplace for energy business in Nigeria, whereby private sector involvement was ultimately encouraged, and NERC, as a government agency, plays the role of regulator and policymaker. With the reform, the generating dams and stations, distribution and transmission lines were outright sold, partially sold or, in some cases, on long-term concession to private companies, and this finally led to the emergence of 11 distribution companies (DisCos) and six generating companies (GenCos) and a transmission company in the country. However, the transmission company still remains wholly under government ownership. Aside from the unbundling of PHCN, the reform further gives room for private sector participation under the IPP plan, and this has birthed the involvement of a few companies' participation largely from the oil and gas exploration sector, like Shell's Afam VI with 642 MW, Agip's Okpai with 480 MW etc. The reform further encourages renewable energies like solar power, which many private companies have invested in as an alternative source of energy for consumers, different from DisCos and GenCos' operations. So far, the country has witnessed a level of improvement in power generation, transmission and distribution, but the dream of a 40,000 MW generating capacity reform by 2020 has not been realised.

About Skyville

Skyville Company Limited is a leading solar energy company founded in 2019 with its headquarters based in Lagos, Nigeria. The organisation specialises in solar equipment manufacturing and distribution, including inverters, solar panels, UPS and solar batteries. Skyville's flagship brand, known as 'Kärtel,' is recognised nationwide for its resilient quality and reliability for a wide range of domestic and commercial solar applications.

The Case of Skyville Ltd.: Product Decisions

Typically, the Nigerian market is largely import-oriented, and this is no exception with renewable energy products, specifically solar power panels and other accessories. Hence, all the firms in the industry source their products from manufacturers in China, India, and the EU based on business alliances like partnering, business representatives and agencies, direct import and contract manufacture for the batteries. Specifically, Skyville Company Ltd. operates on direct import, a 'buyer and seller arrangement' from a renowned manufacturer based in Foshan, Guangdong, China, according to Mr. Ola, the CEO. Skyville's product decisions are influenced by the following:

Adaptation: The company at the initial stage imported the panels and other accessories, especially the battery, from India, but the need to adapt to the buying patterns and behaviours of Nigerians informed Skyville Management's decision to switch to a Chinese manufacturer. Specifically, while solar power installation from India required more batteries and subsequently became more expensive for Nigerians to afford, the Chinese manufacturers recognise this problem; hence, they develop installations that require fewer batteries, which means more Naira savings for Nigeria. For instance, where five batteries are needed for India's installation, the Chinese manufacturer has provided the option of two batteries for the same capacity. This singular adaptation factor to the Nigerian market influenced Skyville's decision to shift its import base to China. It is important to note that the battery is the most critical part of the solar power installation; while other accessories like panels can be sourced from other markets, the need to enjoy economies of scale and reduce related costs in importation further made Skyville concentrate all business in China.

Target Market: Presently, the largest demand for solar power comes from household users, and the segment remains vibrant for the industry. This segment can further be classified according to geographical locations: urban, semi-urban and rural areas. The elites in urban areas and their associated economic activities around the major cities are characterised by huge energy demand to power their homes and mega businesses, but are usually underserved by the electricity distribution companies. Consumers in this category (also called 'Maximum Demand Customers') possess high purchasing power and the willingness to pay just to enjoy a consistent electricity supply around the clock.

Similarly, semi-urban dwellers also have relatively high energy demand but are also underserved. You may find some middle-class artisans, small-scale businesses etc. around these areas. Rural area dwellers typically have the lowest energy demand and are therefore not so attractive for electricity distribution companies, given the fact that infrastructure investments would take a longer time to recover since consumers here lack deep pockets generally. Hence, rural dwellers are either grossly underserved or without access at all. It is estimated that about 80% of Nigerians do not have access to electricity.

Buying Power: The buying power is higher in the southern market than in the northern market. This is not strange to business operations in the country; like other sectors and industries of the economy, the purchasing power is usually higher in the southern part of Nigeria. The development may not be unconnected to the concentration of many economic activities and powers in the southern cities like Lagos, Port Harcourt, Onitsha, Ibadan, Abba etc. The GINI Coefficient Index (2022) shows that Nigeria's income inequality index improves from 1985's 38.7% and 1996's 51.9% to 35.1% in 2022, and this makes Nigeria 11th in West Africa and 100th out of 163 countries in the table (NairaMetric, 2023). However, the income gap between the South and the North remains huge due to socio-economic and developmental factors. According to the Centre for Global Development's (CGD, 2018) publication, the charts revealed that the disparity between the two regions got worsened in 2004 when the poverty index in the South stood at 36.5 and the North at 64.2, and 53.9 and 73.9 in 2010, respectively. The reasons for the huge disparity were alluded to factors like the level of adult literacy, which is higher in the South than in the North. For instance, the number of universities per region grew from 14 in the North and 17 in the South in 1990 to 58 in the North and 102 in the South in 2017. Also, the ravaging herdsmen attack and banditry are more pronounced in the north than in the south, which has made many people lose their sources of livelihood. CGD's (2018) report furthers that as of 2018, state spending per citizen in the North region stood at $78.10 and in the South was $181.99. By and large, Skyville expects higher turnover and sales from the southern parts of the country.

Promotion Decisions

The strategic roles of product promotion are of vital importance to the industry, especially when one considers the characteristics that surround solar power energy in Nigeria – an existing product in a new market; technical education to understand the usage and functions; a better alternative to enjoy uninterrupted power supply etc. Thus, it becomes imperative to make strategic decisions on both the messages and mediums for market penetration and sustainability. Having a full understanding and knowledge of the Nigerian market, where fabrications and unsubstantiated information thrive easily, it is important to get the right information through the right medium for consumers' digestion and usage. Thus, Skyville Ltd. employs the following media to reach the market:

- The **social network** is found to be the most effective and rewarding in the industry. It strategically provides a platform for salesmen's socialisation, whereby all avenues to meet the right and target consumers are explored. For instance, membership in some exclusive clubs in social and religious circles was tapped into. It is not just any club but also clubs measured on the benchmarks of high personal income level, middle and high social status, occupation and education of members that garner good incomes.
- **SMM (social media marketing)** is also tapped into from the initial take-off of the organisation because it is cheaper and has the potential for wider coverage for the target market. Thus, Twitter, Facebook and Instagram were all employed with staff dedicated to handling the operations. So, with this, messages were

updated regularly, and consumers' enquiries were handled promptly with no delay. According to the CEO, 'experiences have shown that many SMEs and Start-ups fail to harness the potentials of SMM because the responsibilities of handling SMM is given to staff who equally handle other responsibilities within the organisation, hence chats, enquiries and requests from clients or prospects are left unattended to for days, even weeks.' This abnormality easily makes clients and prospects look for or switch to competitors' brands.

- **Stores/outlets branding** takes the form of painting or redesigning the exteriors of the intermediaries' or distributors' outlets with Skyville Ltd.'s logo, symbol and colours, and this doubles as Skyville's brand image promotion and awareness creation in the market. With this, all the Skyville distributors' outlets have a unique identity and image that makes them easily recognisable for consumers across the country. It further strengthens the popularity of the company's brand and its preference among consumers who patronise the company and distributors alike.
- **Referrals have** contributed greatly to sales. The secret of referrals in the industry is that not many consumers have access to social media, and not many find the information from the sources reliable or unexaggerated. But a testimonial from close associates or friends, when they visit them and see the performance of Skyville's brands, gives them confidence in their patronage. According to the CEO, referrals contribute greatly to sales in both the northern and southern markets of the country.
- **Exhibitions and trade shows** have, in recent times, afforded the organisation the opportunity to gain visibility in the industry, especially with new prospects and existing users who are looking for better brands or reliable companies that have better after-sales services. Equally, the forum provides an opportunity to meet distributors who have heard about Skyville Ltd. before, especially intermediaries who are looking for better terms of partnering in margin and support services. Energy symposiums and conference attendance have largely contributed to the success.
- **Publications** through Skyville Ltd.'s blogs and newsletters equally form part of the marketing communication strategies of the organisation, and these are broadcasted through the mailing list database, reaching both existing clients and prospects alike. According to Skyville's Sales team, the inherent advantages of the newsletter are to achieve users' education towards attitude change and attitude formation for solar power energy, especially Skyville Ltd.'s brands and services in the Nigerian market.

Competition

Competition in the industry is characterised by many developments, ranging from industry factors to the government's regulator-induced competition. The most prominent sources of competition will be discussed.

Industry: The rise in demand for solar power has attracted more players into the industry, both indigenous and foreign firms alike. Generally, most firms are either specialised in solar installation projects or focused on the importation of solar equipment. Although it is not uncommon to find some companies operating on both sides, depending on the scale of their operations, Solar companies in Nigeria can be broadly categorised as:

1. Mini-grid Developers: Large-scale solar projects primarily targeting rural communities or other selected communities. 1MW and above, usually government-funded or through grants and concessional debt finance from global institutions, including USAID Power Africa, the United States Africa Development Foundation, the African Development Bank, GIZ, Department for International Development, the Heinrich Boell Foundation and a Shell-funded impact investment company called All-On.
2. Commercial and Industrial: These are utility companies characterised by integrated power-as-a-service business models. Power Purchase Agreements target corporate/high-end customers, including factories and large residential estates. Hybrid systems integrating solar with diesel or gas to achieve reliable off-grid power supply form a major part of their strategy.
3. Solar Home Systems: Companies in this category typically service homes, schools, offices etc. This category is dominated by indigenous SME companies targeting end users and government projects. Pay As You Use (PAYU), Buy Now Pay Later (BNPL) and solar asset finance are some of their popular business models in order to ease the burden of high upfront costs for their customers.
4. Solar Equipment Manufacturers: Numerous brands of solar equipment, including inverters, solar panels and batteries, with manufacturing plants across India, China, Europe and the Americas. Some companies have direct international offices in Nigeria; some others engage major distributors; while others simply adopt a private label brand strategy and outsource their manufacturing. The B2B model is predominant here, and their target customers are found in categories 1 to 3. Local manufacturing is still quite nascent, with very few players currently making bold moves.

The attraction is rooted in the population – a market of over 200 million consumers, which translates to the number of potential users and households – and the failure of existing power generation and distribution companies to meet the needs of the huge number of consumers in the country.

Europe-used Products: One of the peculiarities of the Nigerian market in recent times is the influx of used products from European countries like the United Kingdom, Germany, Holland and France. The demand for imported used brands or products, popularly known as 'Tokunbo,' across the different industries is based on the claim of better quality despite being used products. Tokunbo items are regarded as having better quality and performance than new brands and products from China and India. Thus, the scenario is equally playing out in the solar panels market and other accessories, which indicates that a section of consumers prefer Tokunbo's panels and accessories to brands and products from China and India. On pricing, the Tokunbo also commands a significantly lower price than the new panels and accessories from China and India.

Local Manufacturer: Recently, some companies started production of batteries locally, and this, to a large extent, causes a revisit to the importing policy of Skyville Ltd., especially when considering the impact the exchange rate will have on the market price. The local batteries are cheaper and of good, comparable quality to the imported batteries. So, this leaves Skyville Ltd. with no option but to patronise the local manufacturers to remain competitive in the market. Invariably, Skyville Ltd. is gradually depending less on foreign partners regarding solar panels and more on the new local manufacturers.

DisCos Regulation: The market has witnessed increased demand for solar power, not just in the quest for renewable energy but also equally to avoid the epileptic power supply by the different DisCos operating in the different parts of the economy. Invariably, power generation and distribution companies have started feeling the effects, especially in the Bands A, B and C categories of consumers, who are largely found in the high-profile areas of the market, and industrial customers. Thus, a new policy has emerged whereby any solar power project that is above one megawatt (mini-grid) needs the approval of the electricity distribution company that covers the jurisdiction, and this involves payment of certain fees to the company. The policy is restricting many industrial prospects from installing solar power for their operations.

CNG Option: The recent federal government policy on petroleum downstream sector deregulation, which has led to subsidy removal of Premium Motor Spirit (PMS) and invariably led to an over 400% increase in the price per litre, is forcing many consumers to look for alternatives to power generation for both households and industrial users. The use of generating sets has for a long time been the most prominent alternative source of energy for Nigerian households and industrial users, and PMS is largely demanded for power generating sets, but the removal of subsidies is making solar power the next cheaper and more affordable option for many Nigerians. With solar power, Nigerians only have to face the initial installation fees, which many consumers find relatively expensive, but compressed natural gas (CNG) offers a far cheaper option, and with existing generating sets in many households, it only demands changing the generating sets' carburettors to make them CNG-compliant. For instance, a three-bedroom apartment with all necessary household gadgets might need up to N3 million to install solar power, but a CNG-compliant generating set for the same household might need less than N30,000 monthly to power the house. In the long run, solar power might be economical, but the initial capital outlay is a challenge for many Nigerians who would have preferred it.

Environmental Dynamics

Besides the technological nascency that puts solar power in the introductory stage of the product life cycle and its gradual acceptance in Nigeria, there are no other related technological dynamics that influence its marketability and usage in Nigeria. However, other market dynamics are shaping the propensity of solar power's adoption as an ultimate solution to power outages and epilepsy in Nigeria, and the dynamics are:

i. **Power Outage:** One potential factor that may accelerate the adoption of solar power among a larger percentage of Nigerians is that if power outages and comatose conditions continue to worsen, many Nigerians will embrace and adopt solar power as an alternative. Potentially, solar energy is not for the conventional objective of adopting renewable energy but as a guarantee for regular power supply for households' usage and businesses. Even the present solar power consumers are upgrading their solar systems to mitigate the adverse effects of continued power outages and epileptic supply on individuals' businesses or households. For instance, the increased usage among the middle class, especially those who are first-time property owners and in newly developed areas, is primarily to enjoy a constant supply of power. The fact is that most of the new residential areas are underdeveloped, hence not yet connected to the national grid or epileptic supply of power where the areas are connected to the national grid.

ii. **Subsidy Removal**: The present government's decision to remove subsidies on PMS, alternatively called 'Petrol,' is a huge opportunity for the solar power market and other forms of alternative energy that do not depend on PMS. PMS accounts for a larger percentage of the source of energy needed to power many industrial and household power-generating sets. With the deregulation policy of the petroleum downstream sector that the present government has determined to pursue without any room for a subsidy, the retail price for PMS is now determined by the international price, thanks to deregulation, and the propensity for continued increases in pump prices is very high. From the present assessment, the other alternative energy that may compete with solar power is CNG, and its popularity is beginning to gain ground among household consumers to power generating sets and among vehicle owners to convert vehicles to CNG-enabled. Sincerely, market price, ease of use and risk-free factors will determine who wins consumers' value for Naira's decision between solar energy and CNG in years to come as far as households and industrial users are concerned.

iii. **Noise Pollution**: With this factor, solar power provides a better alternative in the Nigerian market and a huge market opportunity for the business. It is not uncommon to see notices in many houses and estates stipulating the hours that power-generating sets can be used because of the noise pollution that emanates from their operation. In the same vein, some apartments and estates adopt a strategy of communal generating sets whereby only one set powers the whole estate, or the different apartments or flats in a building. In recent years, audiologists and otolaryngologists have been advising and warning Nigerians about the consequences that noise pollution from the generating sets might have on the citizens in years to come. So, the need to avoid it, or possibly eliminate it in the environment, is healthy and a plus to the well-being of people.

iv. **Social and Status**: According to Mr. Ola Ogunsemowo, Skyville CEO, one variable that makes the Southwest of Nigeria different in the consumption behaviour of Nigerian consumers is that many consumers in the region use the installation of solar power as a status boast. In other words, displaying solar panels on the top roof of a property and having light when others are in the dark without the sound of a generating set is seen in the realm of, or from the prism of, high social status and affluence. Thus, the novelty and innovation that are attached to solar power place many current users in the class of 2.5 innovators in Rogers' Diffusion of Innovation theory. This goes to the amount of kilowatts property owners generate, and it relates to the social value and relevance they get in the community or residential area. This factor has made many people install solar energy in their houses to gain more social relevance and status in society. Truly, this might be an important factor in social class determination in the south-west of Nigeria because studies have shown that the Yoruba people pride themselves on social status and relevance, and any opportunity to achieve this is strongly harnessed (Olanipekun, 2017; Elegbe & Fadipe, 2017). This is not limited to the older generation, even the young consumers.

v. **Government Regulations**: This comes in different forms to keep an eye on the sector and effectively control the industry on the part of the government. One crucial area at the moment is the taxation policy of the government. For instance, duties on importation are increasing unabated, which for the stake-holders in the industry is a challenge to the acceptance and sustainability of renewable energy in society. In fact, according to industry stakeholders, there is no plan on the part of the government to implement renewable electricity generation, despite the Nigeria Renewable Energy Policy, which says that the government will increase power generation from the sector by 30% by 2030 through solar PV, biomass and wind power (NERC, 2006).

Nevertheless, the Rural Electrification Agency (REA), a government agency that is saddled with rural electrification projects, has embraced solar power as one of the pivotal energy sources to improve rural electrification and connect the hinterlands to the national grid. Like other stakeholders in the industry, Mr. Ola affirms that the appointment of Ms. Damilola Ogunbiyi as the director of the agency and double as the CEO and Special Representative of the UN Secretary-General for Sustainable Energy for All, changes the fortunes of the agency positively and gives the country a new chart to follow on renewable energy policy towards sustainable development. One of the testimonials of the agency is the Gbamu-Gbamu village's Solar Mini Grid at Ijebu Igbo, Ogun State. The community's solar power project, built by Rubitec Solar, consists of 300 large solar panels to complete the mini-grid in 2018. This is a good signal to the industry of the opportunity that the future holds.

Conclusion

One question that still lingers in the minds of many investors in the sector is whether the government, in its usual policy somersault, will not change the goalposts of regulations that presently guide the sector and renewable energy at large. A section of the business forum society believes that the government can go to any extent to overtly protect DisCos and GenCos and thereby stifle healthy competition that will accelerate power sector development. Also, the unpredictability of Nigerian consumers will always continue to create mixed reactions in any market; for instance, Nigerian consumers are easily influenced by imported culture rather than home-made sustainable behaviours dictated by local market dynamics. Thus, this can be favourable or otherwise to the nascent industry. But time will tell.

Questions

1. What is the future of consumer patronage of solar power and renewable energy at large in the Nigerian market?
2. What can Skyville Ltd. do to sustain the present sales performance and improve performance in the next ten years considering the market unpredictability on both sides of government and consumers?

References

Elegbe, O. & Fadipe, I. A. (2017). Promoting cultural and social values in Yoruba Nollywood movies. *Africology: The Journal of Pan African Studies*, 10(2), pp. 34–48.

CGD. (2018). https://www.cgdev.org/blog/poverty-nigeria-understanding-and-bridging-divide-between-north-and-south

NairaMetric. (2023). https://nairametrics.com/2023/03/21/gini-coefficient-shows-progress-in-nigerias-wealth-distribution-under-democracy/

Olanipekun, O. V. (2017). Omoluabi: Re-thinking the concept of virtue in Yoruba culture and moral system. *Africology: The Journal of Pan African Studies*, 10(9), pp. 217–231.

www.nerc.gov.ng

Part 5

Political Marketing

11   Does Celebrity Endorsement Influence Voters' Choice of a Political Party? Ghanaian Political Marketing Perspective

Atsu Nkukpornu, Etse Nkukpornu and Kwame Adom

The Political Landscape and Political Marketing in Ghana What Do We Know?

Ghana is a thriving democracy characterised by competitive elections and significant voter turnout. Ghana's political arena is primarily controlled by two major political parties, namely the NPP and the National Democratic Congress (NDC), both of which have held power since 1992. Political parties differentiate themselves based on their ideologies, symbols and colours. For instance, in terms of ideological stance, the NDC identifies as social democratic, while the NPP aligns with liberal democracy. It is worth noting the existence of other political parties, including the Convention People's Party and the People's National Convention. The application of marketing principles and strategies in political campaigns during elections has become increasingly important in Ghanaian politics in contemporary times (Mensah, 2021; Dankwah & Mensah, 2021; Kofi Preko et al., 2020).

Previous studies to understand the political marketing arena in Ghana have looked at the use of semiotics, such as signs, sounds and symbols, in campaign messages to attract voters and influence election results (Mensah, 2009) the emergence of a new form of political management in Ghana, underpinned by business theories and strategies (Mensah, 2017), how Political parties in Ghana are managing their brands in a more sophisticated manner to meet the complexities of the political market (Mensah, 2021), political marketing strategies in Ghana, specifically the factors that led to the defeat of the NPP in the 2008 presidential elections (Hinson & Tweneboah-Koduah, 2010), political message dissemination on social media by politicians in Ghana influence young voters' political knowledge, efficacy and participation was examined using structural equation modelling (Dankwah & Mensah, 2021), the analysis of the acceptability of political marketing approaches of partisan politics in Ghana and make inferences on the effects of ethnicity on the voting patterns of the four (4) Presidential elections in the Fourth Republic of Ghana (Alabi & Alabi, 2007), the influence of soundbites, political media, rationality and emotion on voter behaviour in Ghana (Kofi Preko et al., 2020).

It is essential to shed light on some efforts by scholars who have contributed to the political marketing literature regarding the outcomes of their studies in Ghana.

DOI: 10.4324/9781003441274-16

In 2007, Alabi and Alabi conducted an analysis of the effects of ethnicity on political marketing in Ghana. They found that ethnicity plays a major role in the acceptability of political marketing approaches and that political parties with strong ethnic support bases have stood the test of time. They compared the results of four different elections in Ghana and analysed the effects of ethnicity on voting patterns. They also compared the features of the political product and the effects of these features on election outcomes among different ethnic groups (Alabi & Alabi, 2007). Hinson and Tweneboah-Koduah (2010) focused on expert views of political marketing and electoral victory in African nations, with a specific emphasis on Ghana. They conducted elite interviews with marketing and communication practitioners and analysed the findings using a political marketing structure model. They found that product factors played a key role in the defeat of the incumbent party in Ghana. They highlighted the significance of political marketing for the fortunes of political parties.

Mensah in 2017 focused on political marketing and management in Ghana, which explores the emergence of a new form of political management in the country. The book discusses the departure from traditional party management and the adoption of business theories, strategies and techniques in political management (Mensah, 2017).

In recent times, Mensah (2021) has also studied political party brand management in Ghana. He found that political parties in Ghana are managing their brands in a more sophisticated manner, adapting their ideological positions to meet the needs of contemporary voters. The NPP in Ghana, for example adapted its ideological positions to issues and took ownership of the policy terrain of its competitor party. The party used its heritage and ideological identity to underpin its engagement in democracy and good governance. Also, Dankwah and Mensah (2021) studied the influence of social media on young voters' political knowledge, efficacy and participation in Ghana. They found that political message dissemination on social media had a positive and significant relationship with political participation, knowledge and efficacy among young voters. They concluded that social media can enhance political participation, especially among young voters.

These studies have made significant strides to enhance the political marketing landscape in Ghana; however, they sidelined the emerging phenomenon of celebrity politicians and celebrity endorsements in the political marketing discourse in Ghana. Celebrity endorsements have also gained attention as a political marketing strategy in Ghana. What is not known is whether celebrity politicians or the political parties they endorse win the election.

The Truth About Celebrity Endorsement

Celebrity endorsements are one of the most popular forms of marketing used to promote a range of consumer products and services. A celebrity possesses three key characteristics that represent the desired group (Li et al., 2022). According to Li et al. (2022), the audience believes that the spokesperson is knowledgeable, experienced or skilled and that the information they provide is unbiased and objective. Expertise and reliability are two important factors that determine the level of credibility. The question that most people would like to ask is, Does celebrity endorsement lead to the intention to purchase a brand? It certainly does if the credibility of the celebrity is aligned with the endorsed brand. There is ample evidence in scholarship to authenticate this assertion. For instance, Osei-Frimpong et al. (2019) conducted a study on the impact of celebrity endorsements on consumer behaviour towards brands. The study used a structural formative model evaluation and found that celebrity endorsement has a positive influence on consumers' purchase intentions, brand loyalty and perception of brand quality. This result indicates the importance of celebrity endorsements in brand promotions.

Does this scenario present the same results when celebrities endorse a political party? This chapter seeks to shed light on this phenomenon from a Ghanaian political marketing perspective.

Can Celebrity Politicians Win the Election in Ghana? Reflections on Past Records

The use of celebrities as candidates in an election has received attention in Ghanaian politics in recent times. These celebrity-turned politicians, or celebrity politicians, are those candidates with backgrounds in entertainment, show business or sports (Street, 2004). This has become a popular strategy among political parties in Ghana. From a party management perspective, a celebrity candidate is expected to attract personal vote to an extent above party vote, which leads towards vote maximisation. The question is, have Ghanaian celebrities been able to attract enough votes for themselves enough to win elections? A recall of previous elections where celebrity politicians were contested revealed the following:

Political parties have started considering celebrities as planks to win the support of voters. When a celebrity politician gets nominated as an electoral candidate, the voting decision depends on voters' attitudes towards celebrity politicians as a whole and specific attitude towards the nominated celebrity candidate.

In Ghana, John Dumelo, a well-known Ghanaian actor, ran as a candidate for a parliamentary position in the Ayawaso West Wuogon constituency during the 2020 general elections. He ran as a candidate for the NDC but was defeated by the current Member of Parliament, Lydia Alhassan. Clement Bonney, also known as Mr. Beautiful, is a Ghanaian actor who participated as a candidate in the parliamentary elections of 2016. He ran as a candidate for the NDC in the Atiwa East constituency but was defeated by the candidate from the NPP. Michael Afranie is a Ghanaian actor who ran as a candidate for a parliamentary position in the 2016 national elections. He ran as a candidate for the Progressive People's Party in the Ayawaso West Wuogon constituency but was defeated by the candidate from the NPP.

These previous records have various implications. On the one hand, celebrity status can generate publicity for a candidate, but it does not guarantee electoral victory. The electoral outcomes of John Dumelo, Mr. Beautiful and Michael Afranie demonstrate that popularity does not guarantee success in elections. Political experience, party dynamics and constituency preferences are important factors that influence political outcomes. The election results, in which candidates from different parties defeated incumbent actors, provide insights into the political dynamics and preferences of the constituencies they contested. This is indicated by some of the potential voters interviewed in the street of Cape Coast Municipality, Central Region of Ghana.

Some of the respondents said:

> Celebrities make their name in the capital cities and spend their money in the city and they have no social impact or connection with the grassroots and the communities they hail from but during elections, they are paid by politicians to contest for certain positions because of their fame, that is because we see them on television set acting movies but we at the grassroots we see what they are doing as their profession like a farmer, teacher or any other profession so what we are looking for is their connection with the grassroots and social impact. If they don't change, we at the grassroots will always show them the exit (Rs).
>
> . . ., again, most of these celebrities do not attend constituency and ward meetings so they don't understand the ideologies and vision of the political parties they represent. This makes it difficult to vote for them or vote for the political party they endorsed. . . . At times, some of them declare their political intentions very late making it difficult to connect their past lifestyles with the political campaign messages (Rs).

From the narratives, we deduced some key reasons why celebrities who contested elections in certain constituencies in Ghana were unsuccessful in spite of their fame. These include disconnection from the grassroots, inadequate social impact, little participation in political party activities, a late declaration of intention to contest an election, inadequate knowledge of political party ideologies and vision, and political campaign messages inconsistent with the celebrity's past lifestyle.

On the other hand, the participation of well-known actors such as John Dumelo, Clement Bonney (Mr. Beautiful) and Michael Afranie in politics demonstrates the ability of celebrities to leverage their fame for the purpose of shaping public discourse and engaging in political endeavours. Their involvement can raise awareness about significant matters and enhance voter engagement, particularly among the youth demographic. The engagement of celebrities in politics has the potential to inspire and motivate young individuals to engage in the electoral process. The presence of admired figures actively participating in politics may enhance the motivation of younger generations to engage in voting and political activities. During the street interview, some of the respondents' recount that:

> the involvement of young celebrities in Ghanaian politics give us the impression that politics is for all irrespective of age and profession . . . but the celebrities should understand that politics is a different ball game so making fun on stage during campaign seasons will only make us to laugh but we will not vote for them if we don't see their social impact in the communities and their commitment to participate in political party activities at the grassroots level (Rs).

The respondents are inspired by the participation of young celebrities in politics in Ghana. However, their inspiration can only be converted into votes if the celebrities make a positive social impact in their communities and participate in political party activities at the grassroots. From these observations, it would be necessary to understand both conventional and contemporary strategies that have been employed by politicians in Ghana to win elections.

What Are the Conventional Strategies Used by Political Parties in Ghana?

Ghana exhibits a prominent presence of patronage-based politics, with politicians frequently employing patronage strategies as a means to secure electoral victory. Patronage refers to the practice of offering various advantages, such as employment opportunities, contractual agreements and other forms of favouritism, to voters in return for their political backing. Political parties in Ghana organise rallies to mobilise voters and generate enthusiasm for their campaigns. Rallies are frequently organised in key electoral districts with the aim of mobilising and invigorating the party's support base. Political parties often employ door-to-door canvassing as a widely used method to mobilise voters in election campaigns. Canvassing entails personally visiting voters at their residences and actively engaging them in political conversations. Political parties in Ghana engage in the practice of distributing various items, including T-shirts, hats and food, to voters as part of their election campaign strategies. Handouts are frequently employed as a means to engage and rally swing voters and those who oppose a particular cause or candidate.

What Are the Contemporary Strategies Used by Political Parties in Ghana?

In light of evolving political dynamics, contemporary Ghanaian politicians are progressively utilising social media platforms like Facebook, Twitter and Instagram to engage with voters and advance their campaigns. Social media offers a cost-effective means of communication and engagement with voters in political discussions.

The use of social media by celebrity politicians during campaigns has experienced a notable rise in recent times. Social media platforms offer celebrity politicians a potent means to effectively communicate with a broad audience, disseminate their message and influence public sentiment. For instance, we adopted the Facebook page of celebrity politician John Dumelo to help shed light on the use of social media by politicians.

During the 2020 parliamentary elections, celebrity politician John Dumelo, who contested for the parliamentary seat in the Ayawaso West Wuogon constituency, used social media during the election campaign.

These are some messages from his social media handle (Facebook). On his Facebook timeline, the celebrity politician attempted to solve some social problems in his community. Some of these include: On 19 August 2020, the celebrity politician John Dumelo wrote on his Facebook timeline 'Over the past few days, we have constantly fed the residents of Shaishie who were affected by the fire. #idey4u #isharethelittleihave' (see Figures 11.1–11.3 for pictures). He also attempted to solve a flooding problem in his constituency pursuant to his political agenda. The celebrity wrote on his Facebook timeline on 14 October 2020,

> How long can we continue to leave our West land people in this situation when it rains? When we attempted fixing this, we were stopped, yet those who stopped us are yet to do something about this in Ayawaso West. Take my word, I will fix this when elected! #changeiscoming #idey4u (see Appendix A for pictures).

On 19 October 2020, the celebrity politician launched his campaign. John Dumelo wrote on his social media timeline 'Yesterday, we successfully launched our campaign in Ayawaso West Wuogon. To God be the Glory. Nasara Naazuwa! Mura Son Sakia' #idey4u.

After the launch, the celebrity politician's campaign message was education and youth empowerment in agriculture. On 7 November 2020, the celebrity politician wrote on his Facebook Timeline

> I will establish the Ayawaso West farms as soon I become a member of parliament. We have already started the production of mushrooms and we will expand to create more jobs and opportunities for the youth. The constituency is strategically placed to feed the capital. It is time to make Ayawaso West great. #idey4u (see Appendix A for picture).

On 25 November 2020, he wrote on his Facebook timeline,

> The distribution of over 4000 Laptops continues. This is by far the biggest investment in education ever to happen in Ayawaso West. I am committed to raising the standard of education in the constituency through enhanced learning programs and interventions. Together we can make Ayawaso West great. Together we can!. #idey4u (see Appendix A).

In summary, John Dumelo's campaign for the 2020 parliamentary elections in Ayawaso West Wuogon encompassed various strategies, including social media utilisation, community engagement, targeted policy commitments and a particular emphasis on education and youth empowerment. These activities and messages were intended to secure the backing of constituents and tackle local concerns in the event of being elected to public office. The financial implications are that social media usage by politicians offers a cost-effective way to reach a large audience.

What Is the Way Forward for Celebrity Politicians and Celebrity Endorsement as Political Marketing Strategy?

- **Connect With the People and Make a Social Impact:** Effective politicians often possess the ability to empathise with the concerns and aspirations of the broader populace. Celebrities ought to actively interact with their prospective constituents, attentively consider their needs and gain a comprehensive understanding of the issues that hold significance to them. Celebrities must recognise that their fame alone may not be enough to garner voter support. Applicants should exhibit a measurable social impact within their respective communities. This may entail participating in philanthropic endeavours or advocating for beneficial changes within their respective communities. Celebrities should align themselves with a political party that reflects their values and priorities if they choose to endorse one. It is important for celebrities to closely collaborate with the party's leadership in order to ensure that their endorsements hold significance and align with the political party's ideologies.

- **Consistency, Positive Image, and Authenticity:** Authenticity holds significant importance in the realm of politics. Celebrities ought to maintain coherence between their communicated messages and their actual behaviours. Voters generally value individuals who remain steadfast in their beliefs and values. Celebrities aspiring to engage in politics or support political parties should prioritise the preservation of a favourable and robust public image. This entails engagement in philanthropic endeavours, demonstration of commendable moral qualities and a history of accountable conduct. It is crucial to foster transparent communication regarding individuals' motivations for engaging in politics or expressing support for a particular political party. This approach can address concerns related to opportunistic behaviour and establish a perception of genuine interest in creating a positive influence. Celebrities should align themselves with political platforms and policies that reflect their personal values and address the needs of their constituents, whether they are running for office or endorsing a political party.
- **Grassroots Engagement:** Effective politicians establish meaningful connections with their constituents through direct engagement at the grassroots level. Celebrities ought to actively participate in local community events, town hall meetings and other platforms that facilitate direct interaction with voters. This suggests that effective political engagement necessitates more than mere presence on stage, television or in the media. Celebrities ought to engage in grassroots political party activities. This showcases their commitment to the party's principles and enables them to establish a direct rapport with constituents. Celebrities must cultivate a robust bond with the communities they seek to represent. This entails comprehending the specific regional matters and considerations as well as proposing efficient remedies. Celebrities should be ready to exhibit their dedication to community-based service, supported by a well-defined perspective on their political involvement.
- **Balancing Entertainment and Politics, Long-Term Commitment:** Celebrities should maintain a balance between entertaining their audience and effectively communicating their political intentions and ideas. It is crucial for them to acknowledge the seriousness and commitment required in the realm of politics. Humorously trivialising or perceiving the campaign as mere amusement may not effectively connect with voters.

It is important to note that political journeys are arduous and necessitate enduring dedication. Celebrities should anticipate the potential for initial setbacks and demonstrate enduring commitment towards creating a constructive influence in the long term. Like the previous response, this statement underscores the importance of maintaining a long-term dedication to political involvement. Achieving success in electoral campaigns and effecting meaningful change in the political arena typically necessitate a substantial investment of time, exertion and unwavering commitment.

What Are the Questions or Lessons for Business Students?

1. Do celebrity politicians in Ghana have a significant advantage in winning elections due to their fame, and how does their popularity impact voter behaviour compared to non-celebrity politicians?
2. What role does social media play in the political marketing strategies of celebrity politicians in Ghana, and to what extent does it influence voter engagement and support for these candidates?

Appendix A: Pictures of social media usage by celebrity politician; John Dumelo

Figure 11.1 John Dumelo (a celebrity politician) during a campaign session with party officials.

Figure 11.2 John Dumelo on a visit to the electorates in the hinterland and on a charity work giving food items to citizens who were affected by a fire incidence.

Figure 11.3 John Dumelo was on a campaign visit, distributing laptops to indigent students
to support their education pursuits and emphasising his manifesto on farming,
especially the improvement of mushroom farming.

References

Alabi, J. & Alabi, G. (2007). Analysis of the effects of ethnicity on political marketing in
Ghana. *International Business & Economics Research Journal (IBER)*, 6(4).
Dankwah, J. B. & Mensah, K. (2021). Political marketing and social media influence on
young voters in Ghana. *SN Social Sciences*, 1(6), p. 152.
Hinson, R. & Tweneboah-Koduah, E. Y. (2010). Political marketing strategies in Africa:
Expert opinions of recent political elections in Ghana. *Journal of African Business*, 11(2),
pp. 201–218.
Kofi Preko, A. D., Agbanu, S. K. & Feglo, M. (2020). Political marketing strategy: Soundbites and voting behaviour in contemporary Ghana. *Journal of African Business*, 21(3),
pp. 375–394.
Li, M., Li, J., Yasin, M. A. I., Hashim, N. B., Ang, L. H. & Bidin, R. (2022). Impact of
celebrity-endorsed environmental advertisements on green economy development. *Technological Forecasting and Social Change*, 184, p. 121979.

Mensah, K. (2009). Symbolically speaking: The use of semiotics in marketing politics in Ghana. *Identity, Culture & Politics: An Afro-Asian Dialogue*, 10(1), pp. 75–89.

Mensah, K. (2017). Political marketing and management: A new architecture. In *Political Marketing and Management in Ghana: A New Architecture* (pp. 1–16). New York: Palgrave Pivot.

Mensah, K. (2021). Political party brand management in Ghana. In *Marketing Brands in Africa: Perspectives on the Evolution of Branding in an Emerging Market* (pp. 121–146). London: Palgrave Macmillan.

Osei-Frimpong, K., Donkor, G., & Owusu-Frimpong, N. (2019). The impact of celebrity endorsement on consumer purchase intention: An emerging market perspective. *Journal of Marketing Theory and Practice*, 27(1), pp. 103–121.

Street, J. (2004). Celebrity politicians: Popular culture and political representation. *The British Journal of Politics and International Relations*, 6(4), pp. 435–452.

12 Gida-Gida Movement

The New Dimension of Personal Selling in Political Campaign

Robinson A. Bananda, Kennedy O. Nwagwu and Cornelius N. Wukari

Introduction

Plateau State is blessed with vast natural resources and located in the North Central Zone of Nigeria. It is a very diverse society, made up of peoples of different cultures and religions. In this democratic era, the pluralistic nature of the state seems to be more of an albatross than a source of strength. It can be argued that the politicians have not been able to manage this diversity well, and as is often the case, this results in intensive and sometimes acrimonious political campaigns every election cycle. Hence, some of the events that characterise politics in the state are ethnic and religious clashes, which are propelled by political thuggery to create fear and weaken opposition (Akwara et al., 2013). It will therefore be correct to say that elections in the state are always keenly contested, and the governorship election of 2023 in Plateau State manifested similar attributes.

Plateau's 2023 elections were a mixed bag for both major parties (APC and PDP). But not at the federal level, because it was a minority party, Labour Party nominee Peter Obi, that won the state, leaving the major political parties behind. In the National Assembly elections, the PDP won two Senate seats and five House of Representatives seats, while the All Progressive Congress (APC) won one Senate and three House of Representatives seats. In another vein, the PDP won 16 seats in the 24-member Plateau State House of Assembly, while the APC won the remaining seven seats.

Though this case study focuses on the political marketing strategy of the PDP in the 2023 governorship election, the prognosis is done by equally examining the various political marketing strategies employed by their major rival in Plateau State, the APC, which in one way or another have impacted not only the political choice of Plateau citizens but also the entire political landscape. There are a lot of issues that have caused the polity to be overheated in Plateau State since the return of democracy from 1999 to date, out of which the following are briefly discussed:

Naturally, the peculiarity of the Plateau State environment presented its own problems. Its vastness, topography, difficult terrain, cultural and linguistic diversities and political antecedents (Centre for Research Libraries, 2022), compared with the meagre resources (human and material) at the disposal of the INEC made the task of managing the 2023 elections successfully appear daunting. But one unique feature of Plateau State politics is that immediately after a winner is pronounced and the inauguration is

DOI: 10.4324/9781003441274-17

done, a relative peace will return to the state. All differences will be swallowed up, and activities will resume back to normal not until the next election again.

Constellation of Political Opposition and Contest for Votes in Plateau State

In Plateau, there has never been any serious opposition; the opposition becomes strong only during the general elections, as 90% of them are usually disgruntled members of the ruling PDP who move to the opposition in an attempt to actualise their political ambition. For instance, almost all those who defected to other political parties from the PDP prior to the 2015 polls had, before the gubernatorial primaries of the party, either returned or were pleading to be re-admitted into the party. Even the APC governor who ruled the state between 2015 and 2023 was from the PDP, because he served as a speaker in the Plateau State House of Assembly (1999–2007) when the PDP was in power.

The only time an opposition gave a serious challenge to the PDP was in the gubernatorial election of 2015, when the APC gubernatorial candidate eventually defeated his PDP counterpart in a very tight contest, despite the advantage of being the party in power. Though it was alleged that the APC rigged the election, the PDP chieftains blamed the failure of the party on their governor, whom they accused of promoting ethnicity and sectionalism, which brought about the failure of the party in the state (The Cable, 2021).

It is interesting to note that each of the three senatorial districts has occupied the plum seat for the red chamber without zoning the position exclusively at any given period since 1979, when the late Chief Solomon Lar from the Southern Senatorial District was elected as the first civilian governor of the state. Amb. Fidelis Tapgun was elected governor in 1992, who is also from the Southern District. Senator Joshua Dariye, who governed the State from 1999 to 2007, hails from the Central Senatorial Districts (Ajija, 2014). Senator Jonah Jang, who governed from 2007 to 2015, hails from the Northern Senatorial District. Barrister Simon Bako Lalong, who governed from 2015 to 2023, still hails from the Southern Senatorial District and now the man in the saddle at the moment, Barrister Caleb Manasseh Mutfwang, hails from the Central Senatorial District (Africa Research Institute, 2016). Judging from the foregoing, it can be deduced that there is no zoning arrangement since some zones have produced more governors than others. As a result, there is agitation for zoning by the political gladiators in the state. The development generated ripples and controversy across party divisions in the state. However, in 2023, there was a coincidence that brought about the emergence of Caleb Mutfwang of the PDP and Nentawe Yilwatda of the APC, both of whom hail from the same central senatorial district of the state (Civic Hive, 2023).

Promotional Mix and Political Campaign in Plateau State

Candidates, political consultants and political players in Plateau State have successfully employed the political marketing promotional mix in politics in the state.

These promotional mix elements include the following: advertising, direct marketing, personal selling, publicity, public relations and sales promotion.

Advertising: The major parties in Plateau State, the APC and the Peoples Democratic Party (PDP) used media advertising techniques, including both electronic and print. The deployment of media advertising is commonplace and has been well integrated into political campaigns for some time during the electioneering campaigns in Plateau State. The early use of print, outdoor, and eventually radio and television advertising as applied to politics has been well documented. The intensity of political advertising signals one objective: 'When a short message of little substance is repeated that often, it is clear that the goal is not to inform, but rather to persuade.' However, advertising may have a more significant role for voter information than traditional news coverage because it provides a shorthand mechanism for diffusing potentially salient information (Maryani, 2015). If politics has failed to recognise the full value of advertising, which is indeed used profusely, it may be because political advisers see advertising as an isolated element of the campaign rather than an integrated component of promotional strategy.

Publicity: Publicity gives candidates free coverage in the press, is an element of both public relations and marketing. It is found to be necessary in most political campaigns. Owing to the public nature and potential impact of election campaigns, they are more or less inherently newsworthy. Major campaigns, such as those for state-wide or federal offices, would not normally be able to afford to communicate the amount of information necessary to create general awareness of the candidate's position on major issues without publicity or the so-called free media. For example, during the campaigns, the candidates of both political parties (APC and PDP) had townhall meetings, which were transmitted to major television and radio markets with advance notice to the press concerning the manifesto announcements of their candidates and platforms. Media representatives not present at the event were sent pre-produced taped spots of the announcement. The estimated cost of the news coverage for this tactic was greater than the budget for all paid broadcast media during the entire campaign. Throughout the campaign, the candidates for both political parties continued to successfully use free media with a series of events all through the campaign period.

Free media can also have a negative and sometimes damaging effect. Since a newsworthy story can be favourable as well as unfavourable to the candidate, publicity must be managed as carefully as possible. However, publicity is only one aspect of public relations. Marketers must recognise that public relations is a two-way form of communication (Baines, 2002) if they are to avoid severe errors in campaign management. For example, a clear understanding of the role of the press under the law is necessary to avoid conflict. Some negative commentary from the press should be expected. Campaign managers should look at these instances as an opportunity to provide an appropriate rebuttal. Thus, the reinforcement of positive messages or the rebuttal of contradictory messages from the press must be integrated into a fully strategic marketing plan.

Sales Promotion: Campaigns for political office have also used buttons, posters, yard signs, banners, t-shirts, hats, bumper stickers, matchbooks and other such devices associated with sales promotion. Again, the practice should be part of a comprehensive marketing strategy. Campaign colours and the script used in printing the candidate's name on placards are too often the product of long strategy sessions in otherwise issueless campaigns. Nonetheless, a certain amount of sales promotion is part of the tradition and is to be expected, even as expenditures drop as a percentage of the total spent on advertising.

Direct Marketing: Both the major parties under study (APC and PDP) proposed video and audio tapes about the candidate, which were sent as separate mailings to names on social media networks, contacts and donor lists. Improved computer capability, direct mail software, job shops specialising in the generation of voter lists, and past contributor lists have made direct mail the' fastest-growing promotional area of political marketing. Many of the professional elements of commercial direct mail have been adopted in the politics of Plateau State. Personal salutations, individualised names in the body of the letter, targeted inserts into various lists, return mail envelopes and other elements have all been utilised.

Personal Selling: This can be considered a means of organising interpersonal communications so that customers will be encouraged to use the sponsor's products or services. Clearly, the activities of a political candidate expressed in euphemisms such as pressing the flesh, kissing babies, working the crowds, ringing doorbells, door-to-door canvassing and other personal appearances qualify as interpersonal persuasion. Only in their case does the seller seek to procure a voter rather than sell a product or service. Although many politicians have a great deal of experience in the inherent activities of personal selling, they still benefit from a deeper understanding of how corporations orchestrate personal selling. First, just as a sales representative cultivates a purchasing agent over time, it is useful for the politician to conceive of the campaign process as a multiple-step model that involves systematically developing and harvesting the votes of the public. Some of the critical steps to take would be to qualify voters (via voter eligibility and shaping partisan affiliation), generate awareness through personal appearances and enact a particular platform in exchange for the vote.

On the other hand, related elements of the traditional model, such as listening to objections and post-sales service, have applicability in the sense that politicians should design mechanisms for soliciting ongoing feedback from their constituency. Other dimensions of personal selling, such as benefit selling, may also be useful. This involves matching voter concerns with campaign issues. Some governorship candidates have been particularly effective in influencing votes and raising funds when addressing group associations on issues of special concern to their members. Obviously, it helps if the candidate's platform offers some remedies for the electorate's needs.

PDP, in order to sell their campaign manifesto, took advantage of a personal selling promotion strategy in 2023 governorship campaigns that was tagged **Gida-Gida** (meaning house to house). The Gida-Gida strategy came and overwhelmed the entire people of Plateau State, despite the well-designed and creative nature of APC manifesto documents, thereby giving the PDP and indeed the PDP's candidate an advantage to clinch victory in the 2023 elections to become the governor of the state. Gida-Gida becomes like wildfire being sung all over the nooks and crannies of the state by both young and old, male and female alike, even though his manifesto was not well designed and creative like that of his opponent. The PDP campaign team would go from one house to the next, from a street to another and from one local government area to the next, soliciting votes from the public by singing the lyrics of Gida-Gida songs.

Public Relations: Public relations is a management tool (e.g. press releases, lobbying, product publicity, investor's relations and development) designed to establish unity and oneness among people within the internal and external environment. It includes activities that are built around a favourable organisational image through publicity and community projects. The major functions of public relations are to create and maintain excellent relations with organisations' internal and external stakeholders, such as persons, private, governmental and societal entities. It can have a strong impact on public awareness at a much lower cost than advertising. In this part of the world, most of the activities of public relations involve societal support and development. Both the APC and PDP had public relations embedded in their manifestos, all tilted towards community developments.

Campaign Products Offerings of Both APC and PDP in the 2023 Gubernatorial Election in Plateau State

Political marketing is really about offering for sale intangible products such as political parties, their candidates and manifestoes to voters, who constitute the market in this case. The major parties in Plateau State did a good job of this, and in this section, a look is taken at the parties' market offerings.

APC's Product Offering: For the 2023 governorship election, the APC offered the peoples of the Plateau, Dr. Nentawe Yilwatda Goshwe, as a candidate for the governorship position. The party also offered a manifesto anchored on ACEES, an acronym that aptly stands for:

A – Agriculture
C – Critical infrastructure
E – Economy
E – Education
S – Security

The aforementioned mantra was to constitute a social contract between the party and the good peoples of the Plateau. The APC and its candidate voted to pilot the affairs of the state in the election. ACEES, according to them, is a lofty vision that will guarantee and enable the good people of Plateau State to access adequate social amenities and infrastructure; access prosperity and good healthcare; and access peace and security that have eluded them for so long. Indeed, the mandate and vision of ACEES were to be the binding fulcrum in the social contract between the people and the APC's candidate if elected as the next executive governor of the state.

Explaining more about their manifesto, APC and its candidate notes that the ACEES vision and mandate of their administration would be operationalised and disaggregated with the promulgation of 12 Key Development Areas (KDAs). These 12 KDAs, which were to serve as the benchmark with which to measure their performance, include:

    i. Agriculture
    ii. Infrastructural Development
    iii. Healthcare
    iv. Power (Electricity)
    v. Energy Security, Energy Transition and the Environmental, Social and Governance (ESG) Agenda
    vi. Economic Prosperity
    vii. Technology and the Creative Industries
    viii. Youth and Women Empowerment
    ix. Natural Endowments: Tourism and Solid Minerals
    x. Accountability and Transparency in Governance
    xi. Education
    xii. Security of Lisfe and Property

Further analysis of their campaign message content reveals the party's promise to govern based on competence, character, energy, capacity and political will to 'talk and do' what is required to elevate Plateau and devoid of ethnic or religious clannishness or affiliations. Another part of their campaign was also targeted at youth. With the tag 'GENERATION NEXT,' the party promised to harness the potentialities of the youth to create true wealth for people on the Plateau.

PDP Product Offering: on the part of the People's Democratic Party (PDP), they offered to the peoples of Plateau State, Barrister Caleb Manasseh Mutfwang, as governorship candidate and a manifesto whose campaign message content covers their promises and plans in these thematic areas: peace and security, the economy, agriculture, tourism, mining and mineral development, commerce, sports development, digital economy and creative industries, youths, women and social development, PLWD, education, health care delivery, physical and infrastructural development, road and transport, power and energy, water supply, urban development/renewal, civil service reforms, financing options, local government administration and chieftaincy affairs, legislature and the judiciary.

In addition to the foregoing, the party and its candidate further promised strategic networking with the diaspora and other special interest groups to advance development in the Plateau. They equally promised to make creative and efficient use of state-owned media outfits to unite and mobilise the people for worthy causes and to be a voice for Plateau people in Nigeria and beyond.

To sell their candidate and disseminate their campaign messages, the PDP, just like the other parties, engaged in rallies, million-man matches, townhall meetings, advertorials on such media as radio and television, the Internet, billboards, the sharing of branded items such as T-shirts, face-caps, packaged food items and every imaginable gift. In the face of all these marketing efforts, the PDP adopted the 'gida-gida' marketing strategy that tended to distinguish them from other opposition parties during the gubernatorial election. The outcome of that election removes any doubt about whether the PDP's campaign messages and the gida-gida personal selling approach resonated with the electorate.

Gida-Gida: A Political Campaign Strategy by PDP in the 2023 Gubernatorial Election in Plateau State

The introduction of the personal selling strategy by the PDP brought about increased charisma of the party and selling their candidate during the electioneering activities in the state. There are varieties of meanings attached to the strategy **Gida-Gida,** as buttressed below:

i. Gida-Gida means taking the PDP's product offerings from door to door or from one house to the next in order to sell the manifestoes and visions of their candidates. For example, campaign teams were inaugurated in every electoral ward that is responsible for going from house to house soliciting voters franchises for the PDP's candidates that stand for election under the platform of the party (Jay101.9FmJos, 2022).

ii. Gida-Gida means uniting ourselves or coming together in order to achieve a particular goal or objective. For example, the strategy is to solicit the peoples of Plateau State to be united in rebuilding the lost glory of the state.

iii. Gida-Gida means returning home to all prodigal sons and daughters that might have left because of the crisis that engulfed the PDP and the power tussle within the Party in the state, and this led to grievances that affected the workings of the Party in the state. Gida-Gida is now saying, return home and let us build the house together.

iv. Gida-Gida means our fathers laid the foundation and built a house for us, but some other people have destroyed some parts of the house. We cannot continue to disappoint our fathers by not taking drastic measures to return the glory of the house (gida) back to the initial vision of the founding fathers (Plateau Voice, 2022).

v. Gida-Gida means plateau is one family; the pioneer PDP Chairman is our father, and we must continue to be so. There is no variableness and no difference, and we should join hands to support each and every member of this family to build us houses from one house to another.

vi. Gida-Gida means from house to house, we join resources together to build Plateau State as the lasting home for us and our children and our generations unborn to secure our house against any form of abuse and misuse (Vanguard, 2021).

vii. Gida-Gida means songs, lyrics, hymn and psalms that the people always sing across the length and breadth of the state. It is the source of joy, rejoicing, dancing and jubilation.

All of the above, coupled with the wave of economic hardships that Plateau citizens went through during the APC government, promoted the PDP and gave them an edge over the APC, its competitor in the 2023 gubernatorial election in Plateau State, Nigeria. No wonder a jubilant crowd gathered in their thousands at Langfield Event Centre in Jos, singing and dancing to the multi-talented artist and music composer, **Caleb Mutfwang's** new song titled, '**PDP Gida Gida**' as they raised placards of PDP candidates and other victorious candidates. The new record is an outstanding piece of music dedicated to fans and supporters. The crowd could be seen dancing and shouting the popular **Gida-Gida** cliché, which translates to **house-to-house.** However, we recommend this excellent song for you if you love listening to good music. This song is made available on www.vistanaij.com.ng exclusively for fast streaming or download.

Conclusion

Application of political marketing is sacrosanct at the moment in all political contests in Plateau State as it is across other states of the country, Nigeria. Candidates of political parties must, as a matter of fact, adopt political marketing strategies if they are to achieve their ambition of winning elections. Plateau politicians must be aware of the changing political landscape of the state, which is reflected in the fact that voters are now more politically aware, choosy and therefore difficult to convince. The gida-gida campaign approach as deployed by the PDP and the success the party enjoyed in the 2023 governorship election demonstrate the advantages of political campaigns being driven by clearly defined objectives that are rooted in sustainable competitive advantages. The wisdom or folly of the more tactical aspects of marketing, such as advertising campaigns, political rallies, sales promotion and managed publicity, is only valuable in the context of strategically developed issues and themes by politicians (Butler & Coolins, 1996). The opportunity to contribute to the democratic election process would seem like a naturally important application of the discipline of marketing. In the end, however, its ethical and strategically correct application should be the foremost concern of marketing scholars and politicians.

References

Africa Research Institute. (2016). *No Renaissance for Plateau State*. Available at: https://africaresearchinstitute.org

Ajija, A. (2014). Plateau politics. *Premium Times*. Available at: https://www.premiumtimesng.com

Akwara, A. Z., Akwara, N. F. & Onimawo, J. (2013). The impacts of culture and religion, ethnicity, politics and poverty on ethnic violence in Plateau State of Nigeria. *Mediterranean Journal of Social Sciences*, 4(14), pp. 657–668.

Baines, C. (2002). The political marketing planning process: Improving image and massage in target areas strategy. *Marketing Intelligence & Planning*, 20(1), MCB University Press.

Butler, P. & Coolins, N. (1996). Strategic analysis in political markets. *European Journal of Marketing*, 30(10), pp. 25–36.

The Cable. (2021). *A Plateau Bleeding Non-Stop*. Available at: https://www.thecable.ng>a-plateau-bleeding-non-stop

Centre for Research Libraries. (2022). *Plateau State of Nigeria Government Documents.* Available at: https://www.crl.edu>files>attachments>pages

Civic Hive. (2023). *Plateau State Elections Results.* Available at: https://liveresults.civichive.org

Maryani, D. (2015). The analysis of political marketing mix in influencing image and reputation of political party (the survey of voters in west Java province). *International Journal of Scientific & Technology Research*, 4(11), pp. 101–111.

Plateau Voice. (2022). Available at: problem in his constituency pursuant to his political agendahttps://www.facebook.com/groups/330086500673439/

Vanguard. (2021). *Plateau Archives.* Available at: https://www.vanguardngr.com/tag/plateau (Accessed on 15 March 2022).

Index

Note: Page numbers in *italic* indicate a figure on the corresponding page.

Milton Keynes UK
Ingram Content Group UK Ltd.
UKHW021906160924
448438UK00003B/22

9 781032 578347